M000250634

Empowering Students Knowledge of Vocabulary

NCTE Editorial Board

Steven Bickmore

Catherine Compton-Lilly

Deborah Dean

Antero Garcia

Bruce McComiskey

Jennifer Ochoa

Staci M. Perryman-Clark

Anne Elrod Whitney

Vivian Yenika-Agbaw

Kurt Austin, chair, ex officio

Emily Kirkpatrick, ex officio

Empowering Students' Knowledge of Vocabulary

Learning How Language Works,
Grades 3–5

Mary Jo Fresch
David L. Harrison

NATIONAL COUNCIL OF TEACHERS OF ENGLISH
340 N. NEIL ST., SUITE #104, CHAMPAIGN, ILLINOIS 61820
WWW.NCTE.ORG

Staff Editor: Bonny Graham

Manuscript Editor: The Charlesworth Group

Interior Design: Jenny Jensen Greenleaf

Cover Design: Pat Mayer

Cover Images: iStock.com/mrPliskin, iStock.com/Sono Creative

NCTE Stock Number: 13370; eStock Number: 13387
ISBN 978-0-8141-1337-0; eISBN 978-0-8141-1338-7

©2020 by the National Council of Teachers of English.

All rights reserved. No part of this publication may be reproduced or transmitted in any form or by any means, electronic or mechanical, including photocopy, or any information storage and retrieval system, without permission from the copyright holder. Printed in the United States of America.

It is the policy of NCTE in its journals and other publications to provide a forum for the open discussion of ideas concerning the content and the teaching of English and the language arts. Publicity accorded to any particular point of view does not imply endorsement by the Executive Committee, the Board of Directors, or the membership at large, except in announcements of policy, where such endorsement is clearly specified.

NCTE provides equal employment opportunity to all staff members and applicants for employment without regard to race, color, religion, sex, national origin, age, physical, mental or perceived handicap/disability, sexual orientation including gender identity or expression, ancestry, genetic information, marital status, military status, unfavorable discharge from military service, pregnancy, citizenship status, personal appearance, matriculation or political affiliation, or any other protected status under applicable federal, state, and local laws.

Every effort has been made to provide current URLs and email addresses, but, because of the rapidly changing nature of the web, some sites and addresses may no longer be accessible.

Library of Congress Cataloging-in-Publication Data
Names: Fresch, Mary Jo, 1952- author. | Harrison, David L. (David Lee), 1937- author.
Title: Empowering students' knowledge of vocabulary : learning how language works, grades 3-5 / Mary Jo Fresch and David L. Harrison.
Description: Champaign, Illinois : National Council of Teachers of English, [2020] | Includes bibliographical references and index. | Summary: "Provides upper elementary students a deeper understanding of how the English language works while enriching their vocabularies and improving their reading and writing skills through information and lessons about language"—Provided by publisher.
Identifiers: LCCN 2020003154 (print) | LCCN 2020030155 (ebook) | ISBN 9780814113370 (trade paperback) | ISBN 9780814113387 (adobe pdf)
Subjects: LCSH: Vocabulary—Study and teaching (Elementary) | Language arts (Elementary)
Classification: LCC LB1574.5 .F77 2020 (print) | LCC LB1574.5 (ebook) | DDC 372.44--dc23
LC record available at https://lccn.loc.gov/2020030154
LC ebook record available at https://lccn.loc.gov/2020030155

To Aileen Ford Wheaton (1955–2018),
My word nerd friend and first coauthor.
You had an incredible ability to know just
what students need.
—MJF

To Maryann Wakefield,
For all the young lives you helped shape,
as a teacher and a principal.
With appreciation and love.
—DLH

Contents

Preface

....

Y ou might be wondering why the two of us teamed up to write this book. We have written together before (six other books) and we share a love of reading, writing, and children. Let us each tell you a little something about how we got into "words"—both the study and use of the English language.

MARY JO: I have always been a reader. Anytime, anywhere . . . even under the covers with a flashlight. I was one of those kids who had to go to the dictionary when I encountered a new word. I was just too Type A to simply skip over a word. That love of reading served me well—particularly when I became a third-grade teacher and I got to share my love of books and new words with my students. Parenting was an easy segue into more reading aloud and conversations about words. Eventually, I spent many years preparing future teachers. I always read aloud to them and encouraged them to share their love of books and words with their students. Somewhere in there, my daughter took an etymology class in high school. I helped her with homework (unfortunately, she had to memorize a lot of words), but I got totally engrossed in word histories. It took off from there . . . and now, everywhere I go, I seem to find word stories (or I should say they find me). My husband's car magazine explained that a dashboard was originally a board on a wagon to protect passengers from the mud thrown from the horses' hooves during a "dash." In *Deception Point* (2001), Dan Brown explained that polar bears are only in the Artic. *Arktos* is Greek for "bear." Therefore, Antarctica (*anti* means "not") does not have bears! I share with students, young and old, that our funny bone is at the enlarged end of our "humerus" bone (ha ha) and that *school* means "leisure" (only wealthy men of ancient times had time to contemplate, discuss, and lecture). I could go on, but my focus has been, and continues to be, to snag students' interest by sharing stories about words. I love the wonder in their eyes as they listen. Then I watch the flame of curiosity ignite as they investigate their own wonderings. I encourage teachers to hunt for stories across the curriculum. What better way to make content vocabulary memorable? Examining words, whether it be their histories, a synonym or antonym, how they are used in idioms, similes and metaphors, is both fascinating and rewarding. Welcome to our book!

DAVID: When Daddy set me on his lap and read to me, he used the wrong voices and got the number of pigs and bears mixed up and generally made a mess of things. I had to stay alert because I never knew when he might screw up something else. Sometimes, it was hard to hear him because of my shrieks of laughter. When Mommy read, she always got it right. It was she who bought a book of patriotic writings and helped me memorize the Gettysburg Address when I was four years old.

Guess how many words I knew in the first sentence: "Four score and seven years ago our fathers brought forth on this continent, a new nation, conceived in Liberty, and dedicated to the proposition that all men are created equal." Daddy made reading a funny game that kept me involved. Mommy found ways to challenge me, to introduce me to big words and concepts. She made me think and want to learn more. From her, I discovered that, if I committed words, thoughts, even speeches to memory, I could carry them around in my mind to savor and enjoy wherever I went.

Like Mary Jo, from an early age I loved to encounter new words and find out what they meant. At seven, I entered my "going to be an astronomer" stage. I brought home books from the library that were years ahead of my school grade level. Working through them was painfully slow going but, by second grade, I loved to talk about the size of the universe, how planets were formed, and how Earth (and we!) spin through space in more than one direction and at stupefying speeds.

Borrowing some of that speed, fast forward to today. While Mary Jo has spent much of her life helping students learn to love digging into words to find out where they come from and what they mean, my life has followed a related path. As a storyteller, words are my endless supply of inspiration, my palette of splendid colors, my toolbox filled with everything I need.

> Words are . . .
> the shyness of a fawn's breath,
> the sobbing at a pet's death,
> the last cracker in the box,
> the gloriously tailed fox,
> the sweet fullness of cantaloupe,

the faith it takes to have hope,
the bridge that crosses every sea,
the stepping stones to you from me.

Acknowledgments

We would like to thank the teachers who encouraged their students to wonder about words and provide us with samples of their fine work:

Jennifer Harrison, grade 4; Sato Elementary School, Beaverton, Oregon

Susan Hutchens, substitute teacher; Poudre School District, Fort Collins, Colorado

Maria Kruzdlo, grade 4; Frances S. DeMasi Elementary School, Marlton, New Jersey

Kristi Prince, ELA, grade 4; Warsaw Elementary School, Warsaw, New York

Deanna Schuler, grade 5; Sterling Elementary School, Warrensburg, Missouri

Ken Slesarik, special education, grade 5; Vista Peak School, Phoenix, Arizona

Christine Titus, grade 5; Hickory Woods Elementary School, Novi, Michigan

Richard Warren, grade 3; Kruse Elementary School, Fort Collins, Colorado.

Permission Acknowledgments

"Mr. King Is Not Always Right" (p. 89) © 2020 by Larry Dane Brimner. Used with permission.

"Word Choices" (p. 91) © 2020 by Margarita Engle. Used with permission.

"The Magic of Metaphors!" (p. 84) © 2020 by Charles Ghigna. Used with permission.

"Example" (p. 92) Copyright © 2020 by Nikki Grimes. Reprinted by permission of Author. Excerpt from ONE LAST WORD by Nikki Grimes, published by Bloomsbury Children's Books.

"Repeating Sounds in Poetry" copyright © 2020 Kenn Nesbitt. All Rights Reserved.

"Choice Words" (p. 93) © 2020 by Obert Skye. Used with permission.

"Poetry Fridays" © 2018 by Janet S. Wong, from GREAT MORNING! POEMS FOR SCHOOL LEADERS TO READ ALOUD by Sylvia Vardell & Janet Wong (Pomelo Books)

"A Personal Story" (p. 86) © 2020 by Jane Yolen. Used with permission.

Power Up Vocabulary Teaching and Learning

Vocabulary is a matter of word-building as well as word-using.

—*David Crystal*

This is not a "get the word list, memorize the spellings and definitions, take the Friday test" kind of book. It is a book with which teachers empower their students' knowledge of words through engaging ways to build vocabulary. We believe student interest in words can be sparked by offering new ways to develop a deeper understanding of how language works. Teachers can enhance their vocabularies and improve reading and writing skills. But the number of words students need to learn *and* have command of can be overwhelming. How can we make the learning manageable when there are so many words in English? Consider these facts:

- There are around 200,000 words in the dictionary (and, if you look at the unabridged *Oxford English Dictionary*, you will find 450,000).
- Some words (such as *sister* and *window*) have been in the English language since the days when the Norse warriors sailed to Britannia (now known as England).
- Some words (such as *unibrow* and *hangry*) have only recently been added to the dictionary. In fact, new words are added to the Oxford and Merriam-Webster English dictionaries each year, based on their repeated use in media.

We must find ways to help students face the challenge of learning and remembering the words they need to be successful readers and writers.

Our task, then, is to discover approaches to teaching vocabulary that actually embrace the oddities in our language. For instance, words change over time and acquire new definitions. Back in the days of rail travel, we use to say *car*, but, once the automobile was invented, we changed that to *railroad car*. Definitions expand—a *mouse* was a small rodent, but now has a technology definition. And words can have multiple, diverse meanings—*novel* can be a book or a new or unusual approach to doing something (such as this book for teaching vocabulary). How do we address all these aspects of vocabulary teaching? To begin thinking about our teaching approach, choose your favorite activity of the following two:

- *Activity A.* Memorize the spelling and definition of the following ten words from our study of explorers:

  1. *expedition*—"a journey, voyage, or excursion undertaken for a specific purpose" (Merriam-Webster, 1993a)

  2. *coconut*—"the fruit of the coconut palm that is a drupe consisting of an outer fibrous husk that yields coir and a large nut containing the thick edible meat and, in the fresh fruit, a clear fluid called coconut milk" (Merriam-Webster, 1993b)

  3. . . . and so on. (P.S. Test on Friday!)

- *Activity B.* Read the following two word histories. Tell (or read aloud) these stories to four classmates. Listen to four classmates tell stories about their two words until you have heard all eight stories. Add those words to the sheet provided (be certain to spell them correctly) and record a few key words to remember each one's history and meaning.

  1. *Expedition*—This word's beginnings are in the Latin prefixes *ex-* (meaning "out"; think of the word *exit*) and *ped-* (meaning "foot"; think of the word *pedal*). At first, it meant to "free one's foot" from a snare or trap. The idea of freeing oneself to go forward was used by the military in the seventeenth century. The word came to mean a long, organized journey, with the purpose determined by a particular need.

  2. *Coconut*—Portuguese and Spanish explorers landed on tropical islands and found palm trees that dropped "pods" containing a large nut that appeared to have a face on it. Using the Portuguese word meaning "grimace," they called it *coco*. English explorers adapted this and made it the compound word *coconut*.

If you are like most students we have met, you would much rather be assigned Activity B, because it:

- involves the social aspect of talking (with purpose),
- uses peer teaching rather than teacher preaching—in other words, students take an active, rather than passive, role in their own learning,
- helps create memories about the words, which has greater impact on long-term memory (when we employ a novel approach, we provide students with a way to best remember new content), and
- raises students' awareness about words in new and interesting ways.

We know depth of vocabulary assists in reading and writing across the curriculum. Particularly, as students have "learned to read," they need a wide base of words as they "read to learn." That is, carrying their literacy skills into content reading and writing is critical throughout their school careers. We know joyful engagement can entice even the most reluctant learners (Fresch, 2014), so finding ways to motivate all students is crucial. The instructional chapters in this book present playful examples using poetry and prose and practical follow-up activities for antonyms, synonyms, acronyms (and many more "-nyms"), similes, metaphors, idioms, and word origins.

In all of the word categories, our aim is to make words memorable, instead of memorized. We believe providing a look at specific, unique word categories adds an engaging way to help students learn larger numbers of words without relying on the memorization model. Instead, we use a teaching model that plays with the language through poetry, nonfiction, and narrative. We suggest that taking a novel approach can enhance students' ability to expand their vocabulary. As Fenker and Schütze (2008, para. 10) advise: "Although most teachers start a lesson by going over material from the previous class before moving on to new subject matter, they should probably do just the opposite: start with surprising new information and then review the older material." So, let's surprise our students.

Teaching Vocabulary

Words surround us. In both printed and visual media, students need to develop a command of hearing, speaking, reading, and writing a large cadre of words. Focusing their attention on definitions, histories, uses, and spellings deepens understandings about words, inside and out, and helps students effectively communicate. We have long known that oral and written vocabularies are critical to success in school. Laflamme (1997) argues that "vocabulary knowledge is the single most important factor contributing to reading comprehension" (p. 372). Likewise, the National Assessment of Educational Progress (2012) concludes:

> To comprehend what they read, students must integrate their knowledge or sense of words as they are used in particular passages to understand the overall topic or theme. Understanding key words that support the main idea or theme and details that contribute shades of meaning further enhance comprehension to create a richer experience. ("Summary of Results," para. 1)

Daily vocabulary instruction is essential. And, as with any area of the curriculum, *how* we teach is just as important as *what* we teach. "Students need to be excited about and invested in any activity we bring to our teaching—and their learning. . . . Not only will they care about their learning, but we will also have made a lasting impression in their language arts skills" (Fresch, 2014, pp. 5–6). We can transform our introductions to and content of lessons if we find ways to motivate our students to sit up and take notice. Take, for instance, ASICS shoes. Most of us buy them, cut the tag off, and put them on. But wait, there's more! When Mr. Kihachiro Onitsuka started his company in Japan in 1949, he specifically chose an acronym—ASICS—to name the shoes. ASICS comes from the Latin phrase *anima sana in corpore sano*, meaning "healthy soul in a healthy body." That's a fun fact, and learning it might entice students to investigate other words that are acronyms (e.g., *scuba*, *Epcot*, *laser*, and *zip code*).

So how did we decide to organize the chapters of this book? English language arts vocabulary standards across the country set clear goals in learning about synonyms, antonyms, idioms, metaphors, similes, and other important word categories. These same standards provide expectations for students to use their vocabulary knowledge to comprehend complex text. We want students to develop a strong and rich knowledge of words.

And why have we chosen the approach for teaching that follows in the next chapters? There are many reasons to get beyond the old and tired memorized vocabulary list. As Lynch (2019) notes, "students who actively participate in classroom lessons are more likely to internalize content" (para. 2).

Our own beliefs about vocabulary instruction guided the format of this book. In particular, we believe instruction should:

• actively engage students,

- invoke curiosity, moving students from supportive learning to self-motivated exploration,
- encourage a discovery of the relevance of vocabulary learning,
- allow students to demonstrate individual competence, and
- encourage a community of learners to engage in peer-to-peer learning.

You will find the chapters that follow all tap into each of these five elements. The activities require active engagement. Many of the activities ask students to investigate together, thus building a community of learners. There are often choices of how to apply the knowledge they learned in new situations, thus showing individual competence. Some choices will provide opportunity for discovery about the language that can make lasting impressions on learners. And all will help students apply their learning. For instance, when writing, we often are trying to find that "just right" word to describe a setting or character—your students will see that synonyms help us do that! Sometimes, we wrestle with opposite ideas—students will discover that antonyms can help better describe what they are thinking! Expanding knowledge of similes and metaphors can make students smart consumers, as these phrases abound in advertising:

- "Like a good neighbor, State Farm is there!" (insurance provider)
- Built "like a rock" (Chevrolet trucks)
- "Sometimes you feel like a nut / sometimes you don't" (Mounds and Almond Joy candy bars)
- "For skin as smooth as a peach" (Olay Pro-X skin cream)

And similar phrases are in the movies we watch and songs we hear:

- "My mom always said life was like a box of chocolates. You never know what you're gonna get." (*Forrest Gump*, 1994)
- "And every task you undertake / Becomes a piece of cake" (*Mary Poppins*, 1964)
- "Clap along if you feel like a room without a roof" ("Happy," Pharrell Williams, 2013)
- "Do you ever feel like a plastic bag? / Drifting through the wind" ("Firework," Katy Perry, 2010)
- "It's been a hard day's night / And I've been working like a dog" ("Hard Day's Night," The Beatles, 1964)

Relevance of what they are learning is evident when we see advertisers offer a play on idioms—for years, Morton Salt has told us "when it rains, it pours," while the Sanyo underwater camera is "the tip of the iceberg." And, similar to the story of ASICS, word histories will easily invoke curiosity. Once students are motivated through these activities, we believe they can learn new words in many unique and fast-paced ways.

Vocabulary Studies

Vocabulary development plays a critical role in literacy and content area learning. The more words a student knows, the better their reading comprehension will be (Blachowicz, Fisher, Ogle, & Watts-Taffe, 2006). Vocabulary instruction, therefore, is particularly important for students who struggle with reading. Learners possess four vocabularies: listening, speaking, reading, and writing. When children first begin school, their listening vocabulary dominates. While this is their largest vocabulary for a while, it is soon followed by speaking, reading, and writing vocabularies. Reading comprehension relies on students' knowledge of nuances of language and the implicit as well as explicit definitions of words. Writing demands both breadth and depth of vocabulary in order to best express ideas and concepts.

Traditional vocabulary instruction is often highly dependent on a memorization model. Activities that encourage deep processing challenge students to move beyond memorization and increase their ability to learn and retain words through direct and indirect means (National Institute of Child Health and Human Development, 2000). Teachers must consider multiple approaches to actively engage all students in learning new words.

Berne and Blachowicz (2008) suggest that vocabulary instruction may be problematic because many teachers are not "confident about best practice in vocabulary instruction and at times don't know where to begin to form an instructional emphasis on word learning" (p. 315). Offering rich and varied language, teaching individual words, teaching word-learning strategies, and increasing word consciousness can be fruitful in increasing a student's vocabulary capacity. Such activities give students opportunities to use and see words in a variety of ways. Researchers agree that one important component of vocabulary study is to develop word consciousness. Diverse strategies, such as those that follow, help expand students' word consciousness and bolster teacher confidence that word learning "is a bowl of cherries."

What's Ahead?

Four chapters, forty lessons, and twenty-six independent activities (presented in the main text and in Appendixes A and B). The lessons let you and your students explore how *nyms* are names, play with similes and metaphors, dig into idioms, consider shades of meaning, and discover origins of everyday words. Have a few minutes betwixt and between other lessons? Or before an assembly? Or stuck inside on a rainy day? Grab this book, flip to a lesson, and away you go! The *empowering vocabulary* lessons are for students to use to independently extend and put into action the new vocabulary they have learned under your guidance. Appendixes C to E provide additional resources that will complement and extend your current vocabulary instruction. Appendix C details electronic resources for teachers, Appendix D suggests electronic resources for students, and Appendix E features resources for and about English language learner (ELL) students. And then there is Chapter 6—words of wisdom from eight renowned authors of children's books. Are students antsy standing in line a little too long? Open to Chapter 6 and read aloud an author's story about choosing and using words to make their books interesting to young readers.

Each of the strategies in this book encourages inquiry into language in a different way. Playing with and talking about words engage students in learning, which helps them to remember the vocabulary because of the experiences they have within a community of learners. To offer such experiences, teachers must become *verbophiles*—"people who enjoy word study and become language enthusiasts, lovers of words, appreciative readers, and word-conscious writers" (Mountain, 2002, p. 62)—and *verbivores*—people who "devour words" and are "heels over heads (as well as head over heels) in love with words" (Lederer, 2019, para. 1). Only through their own enthusiastic interest in words can teachers hope to engage all learners in word or vocabulary consciousness. Helping students personally connect to both the teacher's love of words and the words themselves has the potential of promoting improvement in word knowledge (Kelley et al., 2010). Oh, and be ready for some laughter. In our experience, students not only engage in these lessons but also find themselves connected and delighted as well!

2

Nyms Are Names

A synonym is a word you use when you can't spell the word you first thought of.

—*Burt Bacharach*

Names. We all have them—first name, last name (or surname), perhaps a middle name, maybe even a nickname. The Greek word for "name" is *nym*, and many English words are associated with this root. We are about to introduce you to a whole family of Nyms: acronyms, antonyms, eponyms, homonyms, retronyms, and synonyms.

Once students learn about this interesting and useful family, they're going to have fun spotting them in their reading and applying them when they write. In this chapter, we'll go into detail about each member of the Nym family, but, first, some quick introductions:

1. Acronym. *Acro* means "high." Acronyms consist of the first (or high) letters of a string of words that are used to create a single word, such as NASA (National Aeronautics and Space Administration).

2. Antonym. *Anti* means "opposite." Antonyms come in pairs like squabbling siblings. Whatever one says, the other says the opposite. "Entrance" and "exit" are examples.

3. Eponym. *Epo* means "upon." An eponym is a word named "upon" someone—that is, a word from a person's name. We bet the Earl of Sandwich never dreamed that, one day, he would become a *sandwich*.

4. Homonym. *Homo* means "same," but, in this case, there are two kinds of "same": (i) homophone—same sound, different meaning, different spelling (e.g., *which, witch*); (ii) homograph—different sound, different meaning, same spelling (e.g., *dove*, a bird; *dove* into the pool).

5. Retronym. *Retro* means "back," as in some words and phrases we used "back in the day" need to be updated so we know what we're talking about today. Back in the day, we simply said "phone"; now, we say "landline" or "cell phone." There's a difference.

6. Synonym. *Syn* means "same." Synonyms are words with the same meaning. *Ask* and *inquire* are examples. If synonyms were siblings, they would agree with one another instead of arguing the opposite all the time like those contrary antonyms.

Mary Jo: From the Teacher's Perspective

Vocabulary learning has a lifelong impact on our powers of communication, learning, understanding, and applying information. Having command of a range of words deepens a student's ability to read and write. While we can certainly choose a word such as *big*, describing something as "enormous" conveys a more precise picture. And, if we use *enormous* as a writer, we are likely to recognize it as a reader. If we understand that "hare" and "hair" sound alike but have very different meanings, we can have immediate word recognition when reading. Indeed, the study of homonyms improves reading comprehension. Any playful activity that examines the "nyms" is sure to make students think deeper about the words authors choose.

In particular, studying synonyms, homonyms, and antonyms is key for ELL students. Knowing and having command of these type of words is "considered to be one of the characteristics of the highest level of speaking skills" (Kostadinovska-Stojckevska, 2018, p. 29). Of course, acquisition versus studying of language can certainly differ. We must intentionally teach this category of words to help all students develop skills in knowing and using them. Purposefully playing with words will not only stimulate interest in them but will also help reduce students' anxiety when they encounter them in print.

David: From the Writer's Perspective

As a writer, I have to be finicky about my choice of words. Knowing what I want to say is one thing. Saying what I want to say is a different matter and can be harder than one might expect. Readers of all ages are bombarded daily by words. They leap at us from novels, comics, newspapers, recipes, homework, magazines, smart boards, bills, posters, picture books, instructions, labels, email, Facebook, even on the sides of passing buses.

I have a lot of competition for grabbing the attention of my reader and holding it. There are more than 200,000 words in the English language. Most adults know only 20,000 to 30,000 of them, but that's still a lot. Nyms are vital elements in understanding how language works and figuring out the best words to say what I want to say in ways that are interesting, fresh, and surprising to my reader. I want to talk more about word choices later, when we get into similes and metaphors, but this is a good place to begin.

The easiest (i.e., laziest) way to write is to rely on familiar, commonly used idioms, in-words, and expressions so overused they have become trite. There is nothing exciting, or fresh, or surprising about such word choices. This is where nyms come in. At a quick check online, there are more than 250 homonyms listed and a similar number of synonyms. One of my favorite reference books, which I keep close enough that I don't have to stand up to reach it, is my thesaurus. A whole book full of choices—wow!

Mary Jo and I start our book with this chapter on nyms to place emphasis on the important role they play as students build, understand, and apply their vocabulary, whether they are talking to friends, doing their homework, or simply enjoying a good book.

Acronym Lessons

Definition of Acronym

Acro means "high." Acronyms consist of the first (or high) letters of a string of words that are used to create a single word, such as NASA (National Aeronautics and Space Administration). Sometimes, these seem so much like everyday words we miss the fact they represent a series of words. Mom might use Yahoo! (Yet Another Hierarchical Officious Oracle) to hunt for a recipe, or PAM (Product of Arthur Meyerhoff) to cook, or pause to read her latest issue of *TIME* (The International Magazine of Events), then decide to jump in her SMART (Swatch + Mercedes + Art) car to go get some Canola (Canada Oil) oil and Nabisco (National Biscuit Company) crackers.

Purpose of Learning

Acronyms often appear in materials students read. Knowing that NASA stands for National Aeronautics and Space Administration tells us what sort of work happens there. Radar (radio detection and ranging) is used in our weather reporting but was secretly developed during World War II for defense purposes (link this to social studies). Acronyms can also be used as mnemonics devices—or ways to help remember content. For instance, the name *Roy G. Biv* is used to remember colors of the visible spectrum (red, orange, yellow, green, blue, indigo, violet), while *HOMES* helps us remember the Great Lakes (Huron, Ontario, Michigan, Erie, Superior).

Materials

- Acronym Lesson 1—sentences (see box below)
- Acronym Lesson 2—copies of the Acronym Matching Game (Appendix B, Table B.1), one per student

---

Acronym Lesson 1

1. Explain to students that, when you create an organization or business, you can use the first letters of each word in the organization's name to make a catchy word (*acronym*). Acronyms are shorter than saying or writing the whole name or title and sometimes they make it easier to remember the organization. Ask students if they have seen acronyms in texts or webpages, such as FAQs (frequently asked questions), or in text messages, such as LOL (laughing out loud), ROTF (rolling on the floor), and BTW (by the way). If they have, they will understand how the letters represent full words to convey meaning quickly.

2. Write the following examples on a board or chart paper (one at a time):

   - What if a group called National Organization became known as NO?
   - And another group called Movement On Recess Extensions was shortened to MORE?
   - Finally, let's shorten Home Office for Maximizing Extra Wonderful Opportunities Regarding Kids to HOMEWORK.

3. Challenge them with this question: "If the National Organization and the Movement On Recess Extensions should happen to join forces with the Home Office for Maximizing Extra Wonderful Opportunities Regarding Kids, what would you have?" (Answer: NO MORE HOMEWORK!)

4. Under the sentences, write "Define Acronym." With the students, develop and write a definition of an acronym.

5. Now challenge students to come up with their own acronyms. A good place to start is with their name: "What words could the letters of your name stand for?" Use your own name as an example. Or show that FRESCH stands for "Fully Retired Educator Singing Country Honkytonk" or HARRISON could be "Happy Author Readily Rhymes Interesting Sounds in Outstanding Novels." Have students share their name acronyms.

Fifth grader Hinata creates an acronym from their name.

Fourth grader Braydon creates an acronym from their name.

Acronym Lesson 2
Provide students with copies of the Acronym Matching Game (Appendix B, Table B.1). Have students work in pairs to figure out which phrase matches each acronym (answers are provided in Table 2.1).

TABLE 2.1. Acronym Matching Game: Answers

Acronym	Name/Phrase
EPCOT	Experimental Prototype Community of Tomorrow
LASER	light amplification by stimulated emission of radiation
LEGO	*leg godt*, Danish for "play well"
NABISCO	National Biscuit Company
POTUS	President of the United States
RAM	random access memory
SCUBA	self-contained underwater breathing apparatus
SONAR	sound navigation and ranging
ZIP (code)	zone improvement plan

After they've shared the matches they found, ask students to identify which acronyms used more than just the first letters. Why might that be? (Hint: Vowels are often added to make the word more pronounceable.)

Independent Practice: Empowering Vocabulary Lessons

1. Have students investigate the story behind one of the acronyms taught in this lesson. This inquiry project could tie into a content area (e.g., science topics, such as the origins of *scuba*, or social studies topics, such as finding out when *POTUS* was first used and why).

2. Challenge them to select content being learned (e.g., planets, presidents of the twentieth century, state capitals) and to create an acronym with which to remember the information.

3. Have students select a family member's name and create an acronym using words that describe that person. Alternatively, this could be linked with literature they are reading, using a favorite character's name.

Fifth grader Riko creates an acronym from their name.

Antonym Lessons

Definition of Antonym

Anti means "opposite." Antonyms are words that are opposites, such as "entrance" and "exit." Examples of opposites abound, but they can have situational circumstances. Let's say we are driving in the car. You say, "I think we turn left here." I say, "Right!" Do I mean "you are *correct*" or do I mean "You should *turn right* here"? As with any word category, we encourage students to think about the context. Some antonyms are gradable, such as "fast" and "slow," while others are relational, such as "above" and "below." These types of antonyms provide rich opportunity for discussions that utilize making comparisons.

Purpose of Learning

To understand words can have opposite meanings. Studying antonyms provides an easy way to learn words in pairs. By beginning with simple pairs, such as *hot–cold*, and moving to more complex ideas, such as *interesting–boring*, students begin to analyze their working knowledge of words. Each time they work with antonyms, they double up on word learning. Of course, simply saying *interesting–boring* can be boring. This lesson is a quick way to show the fun in learning these pairs.

Materials

- Antonym Lesson 1—"Nursery Rhymes That Might Have Been" poem (Appendix B, p. 100) and the text sections "A Nursery Rhyme Changed by Antonyms" and "Other Nursery Rhymes Changed by Antonyms" (Appendix B, pp. 100–101), photocopied, enlarged, or projected for students to see; nursery rhyme books or websites (e.g., www.nurseryrhymes.org/nursery-rhymes.html)
- Antonym Lesson 2—words cards (Appendix B, Table B.2)

Antonym Lesson 1

Show students and read aloud the poem "Nursery Rhymes That Might Have Been" (Appendix B, p. 100).

Next, show students the text titled "A Nursery Rhyme Changed by Antonyms" (Appendix B, p. 100). Ask if they know the original nursery rhyme

---

(i.e., "Mary Had a Little Lamb"). Help them recite the original, circling or highlighting the words that are now antonyms (answers in italics below).

> Mary had an *enormous* lamb
> Its fleece was *black* as *tar*,
> And everywhere that Mary *came*,
> The lamb was *never thar*.

Next, show and read aloud the text "Other Nursery Rhymes Changed by Antonyms" (Appendix B, p. 100). Review each original nursery rhyme and discuss the language changes in the new version (italicized below).

Jack and Jill

> Jack and Jill *strolled down* the hill
> To *take* a pail of *dirt*.
> Jack *jumped up* and *fixed* his crown
> And Jill *went* tumbling *first*.

> (ORIGINAL: Jack and Jill went up the hill
> To fetch a pail of water
> Jack fell down and broke his crown
> And Jill came tumbling after.)

Old King Cole

> *Young Queen* Cole
> Was a *sour young* soul
> And a *sour young* soul was *she*.
> *She whispered* for *her* pipe
> And *she whispered* for *her* bowl
> And *she whispered* for *her drummers* three.

> (ORIGINAL: Old King Cole
> Was a merry old soul,
> And a merry old soul was he;
> He called for his pipe,
> And he called for his bowl,
> And he called for his fiddlers three!)

Deanna Schuler uses nursery rhymes to teach antonyms.

Working alone or in pairs, have students select a nursery rhyme from the books or websites you provide. Ask them to copy or print out the original rhyme. Then ask them to study the rhyme for possible words that could be switched with antonyms. This is also an excellent comprehension activity, as students must fully understand the intent of the sentence and choose words that offer opportunity for antonym work. Have students share their new rhymes. (These can be performed using readers theater—another opportunity for fluency experiences.)

Jack and Jill
Jack and Jill ran up the hill to drop a pail of water. Jack slid down and saved his crown and Jill came tackling after.

Fifth grader Jobey creates a nursery rhyme with antonyms.

Antonym Lesson 2

Create a set of word cards (Appendix B, Table B.2). Note the last row contains two sets of words that are a bit more complex. You can strategically hand these out to students who need to be challenged. You can also hand out less complex words to students needing more support, such as ELLs. Cut the word card sets apart and pass out one card to each student. Tell them to find their opposite. Have students read aloud their set of cards to the whole class. You can extend the lesson by asking each pair to take their words and think of a synonym. For instance, *big* could choose *large* and *small* could choose *tiny*. Have them write the words on their cards. Post the word pairs on a wall for later reference for students. Challenge them to add a synonym to a word card when they find one in texts they are reading or writing.

Independent Practice: Empowering Vocabulary Lessons

1. Leave the nursery rhyme books at a workstation and suggest students repeat Lesson 1 on their own.

2. Have students create word pair sentences. Students should write and illustrate two sentences that use antonyms to reverse the meaning.

3. Ask students to choose a journal entry or the draft of a writers workshop story. Ask them to copy the entry or a paragraph from their story, and to study the text for possible words that could be switched to antonyms. Have them write the antonyms above the words. Share with a read-aloud, which will be sure to produce some laughs and fun with antonyms!

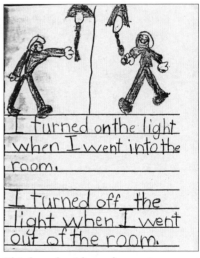

I turned on the light when I went into the room.

I turned off the light when I went out of the room.

Third grader Alexandra creates a sentence pair using antonyms.

Eponym Lessons

Definition of Eponym

Epo means "upon." An eponym is a word named "upon" someone—that is, words from people's names, such as *sandwich* from the Earl of Sandwich. Similar to acronyms, eponyms can sneak up on us as everyday words. For instance, "leotard" is named for the French aerialist Jules Léotard, who invented the attire. Graham crackers are named after the Reverend Sylvester Graham, a nine-teenth-century Presbyterian minister who promoted dietary reform. He created the snack as a healthy option.

Purpose of Learning

To understand that many words come from people's names. Many are related to the fields of science and social studies. Often, the pronunciation and spelling of such words do not follow traditional phonic rules because they are names. Studying these words can be connected to reading biographies.

Materials

- Eponym Lesson 1—eponym sentence (Appendix B, p. 102); eponym website (e.g., www.englishclub.com/ref/List_of_Eponyms)
- Eponym Lesson 2—Eponym Matching Game, copied for pairs of students (Appendix B, Table B.3); etymology website (e.g., www .etymonline.com)

Eponym Lesson 1

Show students the sentence below (the version in Appendix B, p. 102, can be made projectable). Write "eponym" on a board and ask students if they know what it means. Be certain they understand the definition of an eponym (i.e., a word formed from a person's name). Tell them this twenty-three-word sentence contains seven eponyms. Can they can find them?

> I saw a guy with long sideburns wearing a cardigan riding on a Ferris wheel eating a jumbo sandwich and a Baby Ruth.

Next, show the rearranged elements of the sentence, each ending with one of the eponyms.

> I saw a *guy*
> with long *sideburns*
> wearing a *cardigan*
> riding on a *Ferris wheel*
> eating a *jumbo*
> *sandwich*
> and a *Baby Ruth*.

And finally, provide an explanation of how each eponym is connected to history. It reminds us that language is a living thing with many ties, often surprising, to our past.

I saw a *guy*
> (Guy Fawkes, who attempted to blow up the House of Lords and assassinate King James I in 1605)

with long *sideburns*
> (American Civil War general Ambrose Burnside, a man known for his unusual facial hairstyle that connected thick sideburns by way of a moustache but left the chin clean-shaven)

wearing a *cardigan*
> (The seventh Earl of Cardigan, who led the Charge of the Light Brigade in 1854 against Russian forces in the Crimea—the waistcoats or "cardigans" he and his men often wore became highly fashionable in England)

riding on a *Ferris wheel*
> (George Washington Gale Ferris Jr. was an American bridge builder who planned and built the first Ferris wheel as a monument for the World's Columbian Exposition in Chicago in 1893)

eating a *jumbo*
> (A giant nineteenth-century African elephant named Jumbo was the first of its species to arrive in Europe alive—it lived in the London Zoo for many years and was the largest elephant in captivity)

Sandwich
> (John Montagu (1718–1792), the fourth Earl of Sandwich in England, was a gambler who didn't like to leave the table to eat, and, when he played cards, he would place his lunch meat between two slices of bread to avoid getting greasy hands)

and a *Baby Ruth*
> (In 1920, the Curtiss Candy Company modified its Kandy Kake into the Baby Ruth, named after President Grover Cleveland's eldest daughter, Ruth)

Using EnglishClub's list of eponyms (www.englishclub.com/ref/List_of_Eponyms), have the students help you create a list of possible eponyms to explore. Ask the students to pair up and create sentences using the eponyms. These can be shared with the class, first as a read aloud sentence (can their classmates guess which words are eponyms?) and then expanded to read the sentence with the story of each eponym. Post these in the classroom, to be available for students to read over the next few days.

Eponym Lesson 2

Give pairs of students a copy of the Eponym Matching Game (Appendix B, Table B.3) and ask them to match the word with the person associated with it.

Eponym Matching Game: Answers

- Doberman Pinscher (Friedrich Ludwig Dobermann)
- dunce (John Duns Scotus)
- Ferris wheel (George Washington Gale Ferris Jr.)
- Frisbee (Frisbie Pie Company)
- graham cracker (Reverend Sylvester Graham)
- leotard (Jules Léotard)
- Mattel (Harold "Matt" Matson and Elliot Handler)
- sandwich (Earl of Sandwich)
- sideburns (General Ambrose Burnside)
- silhouette (Étienne de Silhouette)

Have students share their matches. As a group, be sure to go over the correct matches. Next, create small groups of students to investigate the full story about one of the eponyms. These can be found using the online etymology dictionary www.etymonline.com. At a later time, have each present their stories.

Independent Practice: Empowering Vocabulary Lessons

Ask students to choose one of the following:

1. Using the online etymology dictionary www.etymonline.com, ask students to choose a few eponyms to add to a wall display. The wall display could

be a simple tree featuring an owl image with the caption "Who in the world gave us this word?"

2. Have students choose one of the eponyms from the list in Lesson 2 and investigate the story behind it. Ask them to create a visual display of the eponym, story, and an illustration to share with the class.

Homonym Lessons

Definition of Homonym

Homo means "same." Homonyms have two subcategories: (1) homophones— same sound, different spelling (*which, witch*); (2) homographs—same spelling, different sound (*dove is a bird, dove into the pool*) or same spelling, different meaning (*I'm in a traffic jam, The strawberry jam was delicious*). Homophones are easier to visually pick out in print (*The bare feet of the bear*). Perhaps the most frustrating sets of homophones for students and teachers alike are *their/they're/there* and *your/you're*. Working with these helps students accurately convey their messages. The tricky bit of this category is the homograph. We really need to see it and use it in context to know which word we mean. For instance, how do you read *wind*? Context helps: *The wind blew my hat off* or *I need to wind my watch*. Context is also critical words with multiple definitions: *My favorite flower is a pink rose; I rose from my seat*.

Purpose of Learning

To understand that some words sound alike but are spelled differently while other words are spelled alike but sound different. Accurate use of these words is important for communication. These often-confused words need explicit instruction and attention. As with other *nym* words, homonym choice relies on context.

Materials

- Homonym Lesson 1: Homophones—poem "Homophones" and "The Party" (chart) (Appendix B, Table B.4), projected or as a handout; EnglishClub's list of common homophones (www.englishclub.com/pronunciation/homophones-list.htm)

- Homonym Lesson 2: Homographs—poems "Homograph" and "In a Jam" (Appendix B, p. 105); handout of chart (Appendix B, Table B.5), one copy per student
- Homonym Lesson 3: Homographs—poem "A Peculiar Event" (Appendix B, p. 107); word cards, cut apart (Appendix B, Table B.6); writing paper

Homonym Lesson 1

Homophones

Read aloud the four-line poem "Homophone" (Appendix B, p. 104). Ask students to tell which word has more than one spelling (*knot / not*). Discuss the idea of homophones as shown by the poem. What does the author mean?

> **Homophone**
> *By David L. Harrison*
>
> Need a word to make a rhyme?
> Be careful what you choose.
> A homophone is simply **knot** (*not*)
> The nym you want to use.

Next, using a projected display (or as a handout), show students "The Party" (Appendix B, Table B.4). Cover the middle and right columns of the chart when you first show the poem. Ask the students to listen as you read the poem aloud. Then, show them the printed version. Can they pick out the homophones? Have them help you, line by line, to highlight the homophones (see italicized words in Table 2.2). Then, in the middle column, have them help you write the correct spelling of the highlighted homophones. Finally, view the right column of the chart to check how well they could pick out the homophones. Provide the students with a list of homophones (e.g., www .englishclub.com/pronunciation/homophones-list.htm) to create their own sentences or poems.

TABLE 2.2. "The Party" Chart: Answers

"The Party"	Correct spell-ings	The corrected poem
I *dawned* clean *genes*	donned, jeans	I *donned* clean *jeans*
and *died* my *hare*.	dyed, hair	and *dyed* my *hair*.
I *gnu* that I *wood*	knew, would	I *knew* that I *would*
sea ewe their	see, you, there	*see you there*
I looked but *yew*	you	I looked but *you*
Weren't *they're* my *deer*,	there, dear	Weren't *there* my *dear*,
And *sew* I left	so	And *so* I left
Two come back *hear*.	to, here	To come back *here*.

1. My pencil is right here so I <u>Lilly</u> will <u>write</u> a story.

2. I wrote down the number <u>four</u> to use it <u>for</u> the test.

3. I saw a <u>poor</u> dog so I wanted to <u>pour</u> some water in a bowl and gave it to him.

Fifth grader Lilly creates homophone sentences.

Homonym Lesson 2
Homographs: Same Spelling, Different Meaning

Display and read aloud the poem "Homograph" (Appendix B, p. 105), having students just listen. Discuss what the author means when the same word is used in two ways. Have students stand and dramatize the actions in the poem (ducking down for the first line, going "quack-quack" on the second line, and so on).

Next, display and read aloud "In a Jam" (Appendix B, p. 105, and below). Pair students and ask them to together complete the "In a Jam" chart on the handout (Appendix B, Table B.5; answers provided in Table 2.3).

In a Jam
By David L. Harrison

He spilled the jam
all down his pants,
and now he pants,
"I'm in a jam!"

He scraped with sticks
and fingernails
as hard as nails,
but jam sticks.

His dog licked
away the jam
and solved his jam
so he's not licked.

TABLE 2.3. "In a Jam" Chart: Answers

Sentence	Homograph	Definition
He spilled the jam	jam	a fruity spread
"I'm in a jam!"	jam	a tough situation
all down his pants	pants	clothing
and now he pants,	pants	breathes heavy
He scraped with sticks	sticks	pieces of branches
but jam sticks	sticks	glues together
His dog licked	licked	used his tongue
so he's not licked.	licked	to lose or be beaten

Explain that words that are spelled the same but have different meanings have different word origins. For instance, *pants* is shortened from the French *pantaloons* meaning "tights-like garment for men." *Pant* is from the Old French *pantaisier* meaning "to gasp, puff, be out of breath."

Homonym Lesson 3
Homographs: Same Spelling, Different Pronunciation
Display the poem and read aloud the poem "A Peculiar Event" (Appendix B, p. 107). Ask students to help find the same spelling, but differently pronounced words (*homographs*). Highlight or circle these as they find them. Explain that words that are spelled the same, but have different pronunciations, have different word origins. For instance, *bow* from Old English *bugan*, meaning "to bend"; from Middle Low German *boog*, meaning "forward part of the ship" (and, additionally, from Old English *boga*, meaning "archery bow").

A Peculiar Event
By David L. Harrison

I was tying my shoelace in a bow,
preparing to row from the bow,
when a dove dove down
and frightened the geese
and caused an enormous row.

A bullfrog sang, as a bullfrog does,
in a bass voice deeper than a cow.
A bass made a splash
that startled two does.
All in all quite a row in the bow.

Write the word *record* on the display, board, or chart paper. Pronounce it two ways and have students help compose a sentence for each ("I have the high jump *record*" / "Please *record* the height of my jump"). Pass out one word card (cut apart from Appendix B, Table B.6) to pairs of students. Ask them to write a sentence that illustrates the two pronunciations. Provide an example, such as *rebel*: "He was a *rebel* who liked to *rebel* against the school rules." Note the various difficulty levels of the word cards. Some words from the poem are repeated to provide support for some students, while more difficult words are provided for those students who can be challenged. Have students share their sentences. This activity is a good example for explaining how important context is when we read.

Independent Practice: Empowering Vocabulary Lessons

Have students choose one of the following activities:

1. Ask students to compose their own homograph poems or sentences in which the word is pronounced and spelled the same but have different meanings. Provide a list of potential words with the definitions, such as:

   • brace—something worn for support/to hold on in anticipation

   • building—physical structure/creating something

   • fine—sharp or very good/money paid to settle a matter

   • row—to propel a boat forward using oars/a line

   • wave—move the hand in greeting/sea water coming into shore

   • bat—sports equipment/a winged animal

   • down—a position/soft feathers

   • second—one sixtieth of a minute/after the first.

2. Have students make homophone riddles (see Appendix B, Table B.7). Use an 8½-inch by 11-inch piece of paper folded in half the long way (each half will be 4¼ inches by 11 inches). Tell them to write the two spellings of a homophone on the inside. On the outside flap, they write the two definitions. Provide an example by showing the folded paper with definitions on the outside, such as "one of us means a story, one of us means something a dog wags." Open the paper and show the homophones (*tale/tail*). You can provide the examples given in Appendix B (Table B.7).

Retronym Lessons

Definition of Retronym

Retro means "back." Retronyms are words that came into use because of a change. For instance, we now differentiate mail as "email" and "snail mail"; "the Great War" became known as "World War I" after our country was involved in "World War II." We often use these without realizing we've tapped into a list of newer ways to describe something. A parent–teacher conference might be between the teacher and the biological parent, the adoptive parent, the foster parent, a step-parent—and maybe even a helicopter parent!

Purpose of Learning

Understanding that words can change over time due to human influences.

Materials

- Retronym Lesson 1—David's story and poems about retronyms (Appendix B, p. 108); "Defining Retronyms" handout (Appendix B, p. 108)

- Retronym Lesson 2—"Invention–Retronym" handout (Appendix B, Table B.8)

Retronym Lesson 1

Display and read aloud David's story to the students (a projectable version is available in Appendix B, p. 108):

A book used to be just a book. Water was water. A phone was a phone. Mail was mail. But times change. A retronym is a word that used to stand alone but now we need to give it some help to make sure everyone knows what we're talking about.

These days, we might call a book a book in print or a hardback or paperback because otherwise someone might think we're talking about an audio book, a digital book, or an e-book. Water? If we don't say "regular" water or maybe "tap" water people might think we're talking about bottled water. A phone is a smart phone or a cell phone. A plain old phone phone? Now we call it a land line. Mail that comes with stamps and lands in our mailbox? "Snail" mail. Otherwise, what do we have? The kind of mail we get on our computers!

Share the following with the students:

Here's how we used to say it:
I spilled water on my book when the phone rang and the mail came at the same time.

Today, thanks to retronyms, to say the same thing sounds like this:
I spilled tap water on my printed book when the land line rang and the snail mail came at the same time.

Otherwise, someone we're talking to might assume this is what we meant to say: *I spilled bottled water on my audio book when my cell phone sang and email popped up at the same time.*

Next, read aloud David's poem:

> So water isn't water
> if it isn't from a tap,
> and a plain old book
> must have a retronym.
> Unless a line is landed then
> it's probably a cell.
> And mail without a nym?
> Odds are slim.

After reading aloud the story, pass the "Defining Retronyms" list (Appendix B, p. 108, and below) for students to examine. Pair students up and ask them to write why the word might be a retronym (answers provided in Table 2.4). For instance, we used to say "the Great War," but that changed to "World War I" due to the occurrence of World War II.

TABLE 2.4. Invention–Retronym: Answers

Retronym	Reason for change
analog watch	watches with faces that have hands, since invention of digital watch
bar soap	since the popularity of liquid soaps
brick-and-mortar stores	to show a physical store instead of online shopping
corn on the cob	once canned corn became available
cloth diaper	invention of disposable diapers
hardwired	when some products became wireless
live music	to differentiate listening to a band instead of recorded music
push lawnmower	once lawnmowers had gasoline-powered engines
silent movie	once films began having sound they had to be identified differently
whole milk	after the introduction of 2%, low-fat, and skim milk

Gather the students and ask them about their predictions regarding the retronyms.

Retronym Lesson 2

Provide students with the "Invention–Retronym" handout (Appendix B, Table B.8). Pair up students to work together to discuss their ideas about possible retronyms that might be created due to the listed inventions (Table 2.5 provides some options). Invite them to research an invention to get ideas of how we might add a retronym to our language. Additional retronyms can be found at, for example, http://enacademic.com/dic.nsf/enwiki/2333597.

Model the thinking they need by telling them about AI (which also happens to be an acronym). AI (i.e., artificial intelligence) is now being used thanks to the invention in the field of computer science that is intelligence demonstrated by a machine. A retronym might be needed therefore for human or natural intelligence.

TABLE 2.5. Invention–Retronym: Answers

Invention	What it is	What retronym might need to be used due to this invention
driverless car	drives car without human input	human-driven cars
front-load washer	washes clothes	top-loading washer
flat screen TV	TV that has a large, flat screen	small screen TV
smart watch	watch that acts like a computer	noncomputerized watch
electric toothbrush	battery-operated toothbrush	manual toothbrush

Independent Practice: Empowering Vocabulary Lessons

1. Ask students to select a retronym of interest from the list provided at http://enacademic.com/dic.nsf/enwiki/2333597 and begin an inquiry project. Have them explore sites that provide information about the term and then write a paragraph explaining why the term came into use. Create a retronym display of the students' findings.

2. Leave the list of retronyms from Lesson 1 (Appendix B, p. 108) at a work-station. Invite students to try to write a paragraph similar to David's story from Lesson 1.

Synonym Lessons

Definition of Synonym

Syn means "same." Synonyms are words with the same meaning, such as *ask* and *inquire*. The key to these words is knowing that they can be used inter-changeably without changing the true meaning. Wanting to make their writing more interesting, students often reach for a thesaurus. However, they must be cautioned that not all synonyms can be exchanged and still maintain meaning. For instance, a building can be described as *tall* or *high*, but the two words could not be swapped to describe a person. A person who feels *cold* due to frigid weather could be described as *chilly* but not *unsympathetic*. Teaching synonyms requires attention to context, as with many of the other -nym words.

Purpose of Learning

Synonyms can provide another way to scaffold word learning. If we can describe something as *big*, why not use a more descriptive word, such as *enormous*? Using synonyms allows students to understand shades of meaning while connecting such words to known vocabulary. Synonyms allow us to think about "register"—or how formal or informal our language use is. We may have "goofed up," but saying "I made an error of judgment" is a bit more formal and exact. Sometimes, we look for interesting words to make our writing more exciting. Rather than repeat the same verb again and again, we may look for synonyms for the words we want to use.

> Materials
> • Synonym Lesson 1—chart paper or board; word lists (Appendix B, p. 110, and below), as a photocopy for each student or projected for students to see; paragraphs (Appendix B, p. 110, and below), as a photocopy for each student or projected for students to see; books students are currently using for independent reading; paper, pens, and thesauri or computers with word-processing tools

- Synonym Lesson 2—"We're Going on a Word Hunt" cards, copied and cut apart (Appendix B, Table B.9)

Synonym Lesson 1

Word Lists

Write *walk, sky, blue,* and *whistle* on a board or chart paper. Ask students for their suggestions for words with same meanings (this is a useful, quick formative assessment of your students' vocabulary knowledge). Once they have contributed all the words they know, show (or distribute copies of) the lists for *walk, sky, blue,* and *whistle* (see below and Appendix B, p. 110).

- *walk*—stroll, saunter, amble, trudge, plod, dawdle, hike, tramp, tromp, slog, stomp, trek, march, stride, sashay, glide, troop, patrol, wander, ramble, tread, prowl, promenade, roam, traipse, stretch one's legs, mosey, hoof it, perambulate

- *sky*—azure, celestial sphere, empyrean, firmament, heavens, the blue, upper atmosphere, vault, wild blue yonder

- *blue*—sky blue, azure, cobalt, sapphire, navy, powder blue, midnight blue, Prussian blue, electric blue, indigo, royal blue, ice-blue, baby blue, air force blue, robin's egg blue, peacock blue, ultramarine, aquamarine, steel blue, slate blue, cyan, Oxford blue, Cambridge blue, cerulean

- *whistle*—blare, blast, fife, flute, pipe, shriek, signal, sound, toot, tootle, trill, warble

Paragraphs

Next, show the students the following four short paragraphs (see below and Appendix B, p. 110). The first one is a basic sentence utilizing the first four words listed: *walk, sky, blue,* and *whistle.* Then, show the students the next three sentences, which use synonyms (italicized below) from those word lists. Explain to students that, even when words mean almost the same, we choose the ones that say best what we are trying to express. Which version do they like best? Why? What feelings do the word changes convey that make the sentences differ for the reader?

1. One day, I went *walking.* The *sky* was *blue.* I *whistled* a happy tune as I *walked* along.

2. One day, I went *perambulating.* The *firmament* was *cerulean.* I *shrieked* a happy tune as I *promenaded* along.

3. One day, I went *sashaying*. The *wild blue yonder* was *cyan*. I *blasted* a happy tune as I *wandered* along.

4. One day, I went *patrolling*. The *upper atmosphere* was *celestial*. I *tootled* a happy tune as I *dawdled* along.

Ask students to pick a paragraph (three to five sentences) from their independent reading book. Have them type the sentences into their word-processing program (or they can handwrite, if you do not have access to computers). If using the computer, show students how to use the thesaurus feature to search a word in their paragraph. Can they select a word that could replace the one they chose, but still retain the meaning? If using paper and pens, show students how to use a thesaurus to locate their word and possible synonyms. Have students buddy up and read aloud their paragraphs in both the original form and the new one using synonyms.

Synonym Lesson 2
We're Going on a Word Hunt
Pass out the cut-apart cards (Appendix B, Table B.9), one per student or pair of students. You can strategically hand cards to students who either need more support or more challenge. Begin the round by reading aloud the first card (the correct order is presented below).

The 7 Steps to Learn English website provides word pairs along with illustrative sentences (https://7esl.com/synonyms), a particularly helpful resource for ELL students. You can use the "We're Going on a Word Hunt" game format to create your own version with different synonyms (Appendix B, p. 111), or revise it and use antonyms to make matches.

To extend the lesson, have small groups of students work together to make reduced sets of the cards, using the list of synonyms as a resource. Groups can trade card sets and play the games. These also make an excellent workstation when used as a sequencing game.

Independent Practice: Empowering Vocabulary Lessons

1. Have the students make synonym flap booklets. Make the booklets together, then give students independent time to complete them or make them available at a workstation. To make the booklet, take two 8½-inch by 11-inch sheets of paper. Fold the sheets as follows: (a) take one sheet and fold the top down 3 inches to create a flap; (b) take the second sheet and

fold the top down 4½ inches; (c) place this sheet inside the first sheet (with the 3-inch flap); and (d) staple across the top, near the fold. You will have four "tabs" showing (see Figure 2.1).

2. Have students choose a word to begin the booklet. This word is written on the top 3-inch flap in large letters. Next, they will write a synonym on each flap (e.g., see Figure 2.2).

3. Once students have chosen their word plus three synonyms, ask them to open the booklet to each flap and write that synonym in a sentence (e.g., "I had to *shout* to get his attention"). When the booklet is done, the student will have the large print word plus three synonyms. They may also illustrate the sentences to further define their word. These can later be added to a writing center as a resource for all students to use.

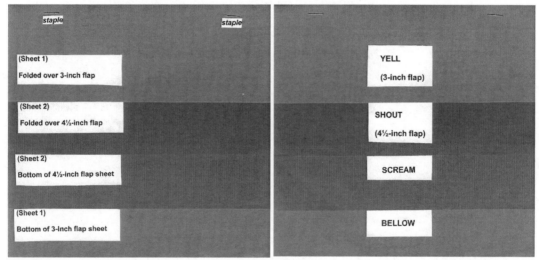

FIGURE 2.1. Template for synonym flap booklet.   **FIGURE 2.2.** Sample synonym flap booklet.

(W)rapping Up the *Nyms* Chapter

Without a doubt, *nym* words provide opportunity to double up on word learning, as synonyms and antonyms are naturally paired; homonyms focus students on the importance of context as they read and write; and acronyms, eponyms, and retronyms abound, and provide some fascinating stories. As we close this chapter, a playful ending seemed appropriate—so, enjoy this "(w)rap". . . !

A School State of Mind (a.k.a. The Nyms Rap)
By Mary Jo Fresch

Thinkin' about learning nyms, what a find!

Yea, in a school state of mind.

The synonym drops deep in my writing brain,
I read, 'cause reading homonyms will keep me sane.

Yea, in a school state of mind.

Beyond the walls of eponyms, life is defined,
I think of antonyms even when I'm unassigned.

Yea, in a school state of mind.

Historic, fascinating eponym adorations,
I tell you, learn those acronym abbreviations.

Yea, in a school state of mind.

Thinkin' about learning nyms, what a find!

Words Are Like Seeds: Planting Ideas about Similes and Metaphors

The beautiful part of writing is that you don't have to get it right the first time, unlike, say a brain surgeon. You can always do better, find the exact word, the apt phrase, the leaping simile.

—*Robert Cormier*

Think of a time you compared two things: the hot pavement to a fry pan, something you did that was as easy as pie, or the papers on your desks were a mountain. In this chapter, two types of figurative language are presented: *similes* and *metaphors*. Let's begin by sorting out the differences between them.

- **Similes** compare two unlike or very different things using the words *like* or *as* to create a new meaning (A is like a B); for example, the fleece was as white as snow, she's as sweet as honey, he slept like a log. "Not quite as strong of a comparison as metaphor, simile still requires the reader to understand the similarities between the two things and make new cognitive links" (Literary Devices, 2019, para. 6).

- **Metaphors** compare two unlike things without any connecting words (A is a B); for example, my sister is a whirling dervish, "you ain't nothin' but a hound dog," he is the sunshine in my life. "Metaphors are considered a strong form of analogy as they assert that one thing *is* another" (Literary Devices, 2019, para. 5, emphasis in original).

Returning to the origins of these words also helps us sort them out. *Simile* is from Latin meaning "a like thing" and *metaphor* is from Greek meaning "to carry over" (hence, transferring the sense of a word over to a different word). By way of comparison, then, *his room smelled like a pig sty* is a simile, while *his room is a pig sty* is a metaphor. These two types of figurative language not only spice up reading and writing but also encourage a deeper understanding of the shades of meaning in words.

Mary Jo: From the Teacher's Perspective

Writers often use figurative language to convey an image or impression—but these may be puzzling to some students. Blachowicz and Fisher (2014) point out that figurative language is often used in high-quality literature. Consider how many times you are reading and an author uses simile or metaphor. A long-time favorite, *Owl Moon* (Yolen, 1987) is full of figurative language to give the reader a deeper feeling about the story: "Somewhere behind us a train whistle blew; long and low, like a sad, sad song" (p. 5). Hanoch Piven's books *My Dog Is as Smelly as Dirty Socks* and *My Best Friend Is as Sharp as a Pencil* are full of similes, such as "My daddy is as jumpy as a SPRING and as playful as a SPINNING TOP" (Piven, 2012, p. 6) and "Mrs. Jennings talks in a voice as sweet as candy" (Piven, 2010, p. 6). Nancy Loewen (2011) uses metaphors in *You're Toast and Other Metaphors We Adore*—for example, "Meet the last piece of Grandma Greta's HEAVENLY blueberry pie. It's OUT OF THIS WORLD!" (p. 5). Metaphors describe or compare seemingly unlike things in creative and often visual ways.

Teachers must consider that vocabulary knowledge is a key element in students understanding similes and metaphors. As students expand their knowledge of words, they can more readily compare and contrast meanings. This has major implications for comprehension. We have long known that "figurative language in written text [is] an important source of comprehension failure" (Johnson et al., 2004, p. 182). Helping our students understand how figurative language is used can also make them smart consumers, as advertisers use such language to their advantage: "Life's a sport. Drink it up" (Gatorade), "You're playing like Betty White out there" (Snickers). Giving students experiences to explore how A is like B or A is B will assist them in having a deeper understanding of what they read. Content teachers can use these analogies to assist in teaching new concepts. For instance, a science unit about the body might use an automobile analogy, such as "My body is like a car . . . it needs fuel!"

When students write, similes and metaphors can better describe feelings and actions in their texts (e.g., "My mother was as mad as a wet hen when I tracked mud into the kitchen"). They can turn common sentences (e.g., "The dog is brown") into ones that are much more interesting to read: "The dog looked like a chocolate bar with a collar." Simple language changes help communicate ideas in playful and creative ways that the reader or listener will remember long after their experience with the text. Lack of experiences with books, not having adult models who utilize strong vocabularies, or unfamiliarity with English may all impede the students' ability to go "from beige writing to Technicolor writing—writing with accuracy and flair" (Culham, 2005, p. 172).

David: From the Writer's Perspective

In Chapter 2, I mentioned how careful writers must be to make sure our work doesn't sound stale. Writers are constantly looking for ways to hold our readers' attention. One of our favorite tools is called a *simile*: comparing two different things to make a description more colorful or vivid. A good simile can add zip to a sentence, but an old, worn-out one has the opposite effect. A wise rule is to avoid comparisons you've heard before. If you can fill in the rest of these similes in Table 3.1, it would be a good idea not to use them in your writing because too many others have worn them out in their writing.

If you need a simile, there is no reason not to use one. All you have to do is find a different comparison. A word of caution, though: be sure your new simile makes sense and doesn't make your reader wonder why you said that—unless you are intentionally trying to be humorous. I'll do the first four on the list to show you some new, yet reasonable comparisons (Table 3.2). The more your students play with similes, the better they'll get at it and the better their writing will be.

TABLE 3.1. Worn-Out Similes

The first thing	The usual worn-out comparison
As cold as _____	ice
As blind as a _____	bat
As hard as a _____	rock (or nails)
As white as a _____	ghost (or sheet)
As smooth as _____	silk
As sweet as _____	sugar
As clean as a _____	whistle
As strong as an _____	ox
As nutty as a _____	fruitcake
As cool as a _____	cucumber

TABLE 3.2. Example Worn-Out Similes with New Comparisons

The first thing	The usual worn-out comparison	A new comparison
As cold as _____	ice	snow
As blind as a _____	bat	stick
As hard as a _____	rock (or nails)	fist
As white as a _____	ghost (or sheet)	chalk

Next, here's a list of goofy similes made specifically to be surprising and silly (Table 3.3), a sure way to add smiles to that humorous piece you're writing.

TABLE 3.3. Example Over-the-Top Comparison Similes

The first thing	An over-the-top comparison
As cold as _____	a six pack of frozen mackerel after two years in the freezer
As blind as a _____	rhinoceros horn covered with a sack of bad potatoes
As hard as _____	prying out a concrete filling with a toothpick
As white as a _____	four-ply toilet paper made from aspen trees

Can I squeeze all of these over-the-top similes in one paragraph? Here goes:

> One winter day, I got caught walking in a blizzard. It was as cold as a six-pack of frozen mackerel after two years in the freezer and the swirling snow was as white as four-ply toilet paper made from aspen trees. All that snow made me as blind as a rhinoceros horn covered with a sack of bad potatoes. Walking into the wind was as hard as prying out a concrete filling with a toothpick. I thought I'd never get home.

Here's something else you can do with similes when you make up your own. You can write silly poems and make them rhyme. Like this:

> One day last week in our classroom
> the kids were yelling like flies.
> Teacher's face
> turned as red as white lace.
> "You're as rude," Teacher said,
> "as French fries!"

Simile Lessons

Purpose of Learning

Similes are often used by writers to tap into imagination and provide a different perspective. Similes liken A to B. These "like" or "as" statements compare two objects that are typically not considered similar.

Learnings

To be able to independently define *simile* and to understand the use of similes to express ideas.

Materials

- Simile Lesson 1—list of similes (Appendix B, Table B.10), photocopied for pairs of students and projected on a board

- Simile Lesson 2—chart of new comparisons to project, student copies of chart (Appendix B, Table B.11)

- Simile Lesson 3—chart of new comparisons to project, student copies of chart with new comparisons completed in Lesson 2

- Simile Lesson 4—chart of over-the-top comparisons to project, student copies of chart (Appendix B, Table B.12)

- Simile Lesson 5—David's paragraph with over-the-top comparisons (Appendix B, p. 115)

Simile Lesson 1

Show students the list of similes (Appendix B, Table B.10). Read the first simile and take ideas from students about what an author might be trying to convey using this phrase. Continue through the next three similes on the list. Note how each simile uses "as XX as" to make a comparison. Be certain students understand the definition of *simile* by having them write it at the bottom of the list. Next, pair up students to discuss the remainder of the list. When they are done, return to a whole-group setting and ask each pair to share one of their explanations. Extend the lesson by asking each student to write a short paragraph explaining the meaning of one or more similes. Post these for all students to view. Or, place the list at a workstation and ask students to illustrate the simile.

SIMILE LESSON 2

Project David's list of similes with new comparisons (Appendix B, Table B.11). For now, cover the "Because" column, as it will be used in the next lesson. Remind students of the Lesson 1 conversations about the meaning of each simile. Read David's suggestions for a new comparison for the first four similes. Next, take student suggestions for what a new comparison might be for the next two similes (As smooth as . . . , As sweet as . . .) and fill in the "new comparison." Encourage them to think about sensible but fun comparisons. Give students a copy of the chart and have them copy the two completed comparisons together and then to make a new comparison with the last four similes on the chart (alone or in pairs). Come back together and take suggestions for filling in the last four similes.

Simile Lesson 3

Show the chart from Lesson 2 to the students (the "new comparison" column will be filled in from Lesson 2) and draw their attention to "Because" at the top of the last column. Discuss how the students will explain how the new comparison shows how A is like B (examples are provided in Table 3.4). Complete the chart together, asking students to suggest a sentence to explain the comparison.

TABLE 3.4. Example Worn-Out Similes with New Comparisons: Because

The first thing	The usual worn-out comparison	A new comparison	Because
As cold as _____	ice	snow	Snow is very cold.
As blind as a _____	bat	stick	A stick does not have eyes.
As hard as a _____	rock	fist	You make a fist by curling all your fingers together to make them strong and hard.
As white as a _____	ghost	chalk	Chalk is white.

Next, return the chart from Lesson 2 to the students (their "new comparison" column should be filled in from Lesson 2). Ask them to write a sentence in the "Because" column next to each box to explain the new comparison (you can also allow the same buddies from Lesson 2 to work together to do this). This is a good time to do a quick review on how a sentence is a complete thought, uses a capital at the beginning, and includes punctuation at the end. Tell them to think about how A *is like* B. Gather together later to have students share their sentences.

The first thing	The usual worn out comparison	A new comparison	Because
As cold as _____	ice	snow	Snow is cold
As blind as a _____	bat	stick	A stick can't see
As hard as _____	a rock	A fist	A fist is hard
As white as a _____	ghost	chalk	orin̑ganil chalk is white
As smooth as _____	silk	sanded wood	Sanded wood is smooth
As sweet as _____	sugar	maple sryap	Sryup is sweet
As clean as a _____	whistle	soap	Soap is clean
As strong as an _____	ox	rock wall	Rock walls or strong
As nutty as a _____	fruitcake	peanut	Peanuts are nutty
As cool as a _____	cucumber	a/c unit	A.C units are cool

Fourth grader Braydon's "new comparisons."

Simile Lesson 4

Project and distribute copies of David's list of over-the-top comparisons (Appendix B, Table B.12). Discuss how he uses strong visual phrases to change the simile. Be sure to point out that he still makes A like B. Together, decide on an "over-the-top" comparison for the next two similes (As smooth as. . ., As sweet as. . .). Show the remaining list and ask students to turn and talk to a buddy about filling in possible over-the-top comparisons for the last four similes. Take ideas from the pairs and add them to the projected list.

Over the top compairison

1. As strong as friendship when a dramatic fight is going on.

2. As nutty as pecan pie when grandma spilles the nuts.

3. As white as a tooth after six visits to the dentist.

4. Light as silk that is fresh from the laundrey mat.

5. As slow as a two year old trying to write in cursive.

Fourth grader Anna's "over-the-top comparisons."

Simile Lesson 5

Remind the students of David's over-the-top comparisons and the ones you created together. Then, project the paragraph he crafted using these phrases (Appendix B, p. 115).

Using a shared writing approach (you and students crafting together), write a paragraph using a few of the over-the-top comparisons you created together. For instance, using David's same four over-the-top comparisons, we might write:

> Finally, the swimming pool is open! I wade in at the shallow end, but the water feels as cold as a six-pack of frozen mackerel after two years in the freezer. Kids are jumping everywhere. The splashing water makes me feel as blind as a rhinoceros horn covered with a sack of bad potatoes. I get out and go to the snack bar. My hands are so cold that trying to get change out of my pocket is as hard as prying out a concrete filling with a toothpick. Guess I'll have hot chocolate! The foam on top is as white as four-ply toilet paper made from aspen trees. Mmm. Delicious and warm.

Return the students' worksheet from Lesson 4 with their over-the-top comparisons. Ask them (and their buddy, if you wish) to compose a paragraph using two or more of their creations. Ask the students to read these aloud (often with hilarious results!).

Fourth grader Rylee's "over-the-top" simile.

Independent Practice: Empowering Vocabulary Lessons

Give students two options to extend their work with similes, as follows:

1. Provide copies of the first "Similes: Independent Practice" handout (Appendix B, Table B.13). Show how the chart is the same as in Lessons 2 to 4, but with new similes. You can allow buddies or small groups to work independently to complete the chart.

2. Provide copies of the second "Similes: Independent Practice" handout (Appendix B, Table B.14). Have a copy of the simile list from Lesson 1 also available. Ask students to complete the sheet by choosing a simile, rewriting it with a new comparison or an over-the-top comparison, and then illustrating it. Share and enjoy!

Mary Jo: From the Teacher's Perspective

Metaphors

Earlier in the chapter, I discussed how authors use figurative language to bring an element of visual impact to their writing. That discussion helped provide insights into the difference between simile and metaphor—both figures of speech that compare two things. With metaphors, in particular, we consider a comparison of two very unlike things. You will notice the lessons that follow duplicate the simile lesson formats. In this way, the students already have experience with making comparisons—whether it be the usual "worn-out" ones or the "over-the-top" ones.

David: From the Writer's Perspective

Metaphors

A metaphor goes farther than a simile. It doesn't compare one thing with another—it says one thing *is* another. My new kitten doesn't prowl like a tiger. She *is* a tiger. Amanda's little brother is a mouth with legs. Trudy's little sister is a stinkpot. I don't think my mother ever sleeps: she's an owl. Dad's old car is a pile of junk. My big brother's stomach is a bottomless pit.

As with similes, we tend to wear out metaphors by using them again and again. My big brother's stomach doesn't *always* have to be a bottomless pit. It's a good metaphor because everyone gets a picture of how much food it might take to fill my brother's stomach. But there must be some other way of expressing my brother's endless appetite. My brother's stomach is a garbage disposal. My brother's stomach is a food processor. My brother's stomach is a trash can for junk food. My brother's stomach has a top but no bottom.

Table 3.5 presents a list of metaphors that are used so much they have lost their ability to surprise. The challenge is to think of other comparisons that do the job in a fresher way.

Also, metaphors are fun to play with if you want to be humorous and keep your reader guessing what's coming next. I love doing this because it frees my imagination to arrange words in unexpected ways and gives my sense of humor some exercise. When kids do this, it gives them a better understanding of how the words they choose can affect what they are saying. For example, consider the "over-the-top" comparisons in Table 3.6.

Now comes a challenge to see if I can use all five silly metaphors in one paragraph.

> It's one of those days when the clouds are what you get when you shoot marshmallows out of a cannon and I'm thinking about my family. My brother calls me a spineless piece of string about five feet long and Mom says my room is the movie set from *The Night the Dragon Fought T. Rex*, but Daddy calls me his divinityfudgepuddingchocolatemintsweetypie and my sister goes through the house singing, "You're my thingamajig that makes my heart go boing." I think my family is strange. I'm going out to play.

TABLE 3.5. Example Worn-Out Metaphors and New Comparisons

The first thing	The usual worn-out comparison	A new comparison
You're a	chicken	cowardly lion
Mom says my room is a	disaster	compost heap
Daddy calls me his	angel	sweet thang
Today, the clouds are	balls of cotton	cream puffs
You are my	sunshine	everything

TABLE 3.6. Example Over-the-Top Comparison Metaphors

The first thing	An over-the-top comparison
You're a	spineless piece of string about five feet long
Mom says my room is	the movie set from *The Night the Dragon Fought T. Rex*
Daddy calls me his	divinityfudgepuddingchocolatemintsweetypie
Today, the clouds are	what you get when you shoot marshmallows out of a cannon
You are my	thingamajig that makes my heart go boing

Metaphor Lessons

Purpose of Learning

Metaphors are often used by writers to tap into imagination and provide a different perspective. Metaphors compare two unlike things where A is B.

Learnings

To be able to independently define *metaphor*, to understand the use of metaphors to express ideas, and to differentiate metaphors from similes.

Materials

- Metaphor Lesson 1—list of example metaphors (Appendix B, Table B.15), photocopied for pairs of students and projected on a board

- Metaphor Lesson 2—chart of new comparisons to project, student copies of chart (Appendix B, Table B.16)

- Metaphor Lesson 3—chart of new comparisons to project, student copies of chart of new comparisons completed in Lesson 2

- Metaphor Lesson 4—chart of over-the-top comparisons to project, student copies of chart (Appendix B, Table B.17)

- Metaphor Lesson 5—David's paragraph with over-the-top comparisons (Appendix B, p. 121)

Metaphor Lesson 1

Show students the list of metaphors (Appendix B, Table B.15). Read the first metaphor and take ideas from students about what an author might be trying to convey using this phrase. Continue through the next metaphors on the list. Note how each metaphor uses *is* or other words to make a comparison. Be certain that students understand the definition of *metaphor* by getting them to write it at the bottom of the list. Next, pair up students to discuss the remainder of the list. When they are done, return to a whole-group setting and ask each pair to share one of their explanations. Extend the lesson by asking each student to write a short paragraph explaining the meaning of one or more metaphors. Post these for the students to view. Or, place the list at a workstation and ask students to illustrate the metaphor.

Lilly

You're a chicken. ☆	
Scared of everything	
Mom says my room is a compost heap.	
Very messy	
Daddy calls me his angel. ☆	
perfect/favorite	
Today the clouds are balls of cotton.	
Clouds look like cotton	
You are my sunshine. ☆	
favorite/special	
Life is a roller coaster. ☆	
Fun	
Her brain is a computer. ☆	
very smart	
My big brother is a couch potato. ☆	
on the couch a lot	
He is a walking dictionary.	
very good speech	

Fifth grader Lilly defines metaphors.

Metaphor Lesson 2

Project David's list of metaphors with new comparisons (Appendix B, Table B.16). Cover the "Because" column, as it will be used in the next lesson. Remind students of the Lesson 1 conversations about the meaning of the first four metaphors. Next, take their suggestions for what a new comparison might be for the next two metaphors (You are my . . ., Life is . . .). Encourage them to think about sensible but fun comparisons.

Give students a copy of the chart and have them copy the two completed together and then make a new comparison with the last three metaphors on the chart (alone or in pairs). Come back together and take suggestions for filling in the last three metaphors.

Metaphor Lesson 3

Show the chart from Lesson 2 to the students (the "new comparison" column will be filled in from Lesson 2) and point out "Because" at the top of the last column. Discuss how the students should explain how the new comparison shows how A is B (examples provided in Table 3.7). Complete the chart together, asking students to suggest a sentence to explain the comparison.

TABLE 3.7. Example Worn-Out Metaphors with New Comparisons: Because

The first thing	The usual worn-out comparison	A new comparison	Because
You're a	chicken	cowardly lion	In the *Wizard of Oz*, the lion was afraid of everything and chickens are afraid of people when they get too close.
Mom says my room is a	disaster	compost heap	A compost heap is a messy pile of stuff and a disaster is usually something that is very messy.
Daddy calls me his	angel	sweet thang	Sweet thang is a slang term for someone who is nice, which is similar to an angel.
Today, the clouds are	balls of cotton	cream puffs	Cream puffs have a white fluffy filling and cotton balls are white and fluffy.

Next, return the chart from Lesson 2 to the students (their "new comparison" column should be filled in from Lesson 2). Ask them to write a sentence in the "Because" column next to each box to explain the new comparison (you can also allow the same buddies from Lesson 2 to work together to do this). This is a good time to present a quick review on how a sentence is a complete thought and uses a capital at the beginning and punctuation at the end. Tell students to think about how A *is* B. Gather together later to have students share their sentences.

Metaphor Lesson 4

Project and distribute copies of David's list of "over-the-top comparisons" (Appendix B, Table B.17). Discuss how he uses descriptive phrases to change the metaphor. Be sure to point out that he still picks an idea to show that A is B. Together, decide on an over-the-top comparison for the next metaphor. Show the remaining list and ask students to turn and talk to a buddy about it and fill in possible over-the-top comparisons for the last three metaphors. Take ideas from the pairs and add them to the projected list.

Metaphor Lesson 5

Remind the students of David's over-the-top comparisons and the ones you created together. Then, project the paragraph he crafted using these phrases (Appendix B, p. 121).

Using a shared writing approach (you and students crafting together), write a paragraph using a few of the over-the-top comparisons you created together. For instance, using David's same five over-the-top comparisons, we might write:

Today started out as such a great day! My friend and I were lying in my treehouse and we noticed the clouds are what you get when you shoot marshmallows out of a cannon. My Granny called and told me, "You are my thingamajig that makes my heart go boing!" I love how crazy Granny can be. As I skipped around the kitchen, Dad called me his "divinityfudgepuddingchocolatemintsweetypie." Not sure what that is, but it sure sounds sweet! Just as I was feeling nothing could go wrong, my brother gave me a push and said I was a "spineless piece of string about five feet long." What? "I'm telling Mom," I yelled. I turned to see her walking into the kitchen. "I've just been upstairs and your room is the movie set from *The Night the Dragon Fought T. Rex*," she said. Geez, I better go back into my treehouse!

Return the students' worksheet from Lesson 4 with their "over-the-top comparisons." Ask them (and their buddy, if you wish) to compose a paragraph using two or more of their creations. Ask the students to read these aloud (again, expect hilarious results!).

A Raven's feathers are as black as a
Midnight sky.
jewlery
Black ~~gems~~ is as bumpy as coal, ~~in~~ ~~~~
The taste of blackberries are tart like
    apple pie
The Midnight sky is a black leopard's fur

A black thunder cloud is like y see fall your
life flesh before your eyes!
A burnt marshmallow is as crackly as grass
Black puppies are as dark as a crow
Jewlery can melt like a crayon

Third grader Kamdyn creates similes and metaphors.

Independent Practice: Empowering Vocabulary Lessons

Give students two options to extend their work with metaphors.

1. Provide copies of the first "Metaphors: Independent Practice" handout
   (Appendix B, Table B.18). Show how the chart is the same as in Lessons 2
   to 4, but with new metaphors. You can allow buddies or small groups to
   work independently to complete the chart.

2. Provide copies of the second "Metaphors: Independent Practice" handout
   (Appendix B, Table B.19). Have a copy of the metaphor list from Lesson 1
   also available. Ask students to complete the sheet by choosing a metaphor,
   rewriting it with a new comparison or an over-the-top comparison, and
   then illustrating it. Share and enjoy!

Planting the Seeds

These simile and metaphor exercises bring the idea of figurative language to the forefront for your students. When they read, they will be more aware of an author's use of figurative language to enrich their content. As Hansen et al. (2011) note, "Metaphors can be powerful aids in education because they help learners begin to understand novel concepts" (p. 1). When they write, they can infuse similes or metaphors to make their writing more colorful. One final idea for the classroom: have a "Morning Figurative Language Challenge" by showing a simile or metaphor each day. Project it on a screen or write it on a chart that the students can see as they enter the room. Suggest they think about the meaning until everyone settles in. Then, a quick conversation about it will bring the meaning to clarity. Here are a few to get you started:

- It was as cheap as dirt.
- Her tears flowed like a river.
- The thunder was like a bowling alley.
- Ben's temper is like a volcano!
- The wind was a howling wolf.
- The road ahead was a ribbon across the desert.
- The test was a piece of cake.
- She is afraid of her own shadow.

As meaning is best conveyed in context, an extension of the Morning Figurative Language Challenge is to ask students to compose a paragraph using the simile or metaphor of the day. What is the story around "cheap as dirt" or "a howling wolf"? Post these for students to share and enjoy—you are a gardener; plant away!

Raining Cats and Dogs: Idioms Have Deep Meaning

4

Man does not live by words alone, despite the fact that sometimes he has to eat them.

—*Adlai E. Stevenson*

In making his point, Adlai Stevenson used a very old idiom we regularly hear—*eat your words*. Of course, words don't fall out of our mouths like objects that can be picked up and swallowed. No, this idiom comes from 1373 CE, when Pope Gregory XI sent two emissaries, bearing a parchment, to inform Count Bernarbò Visconti of his excommunication from the Catholic Church. Enraged, Visconti arrested the emissaries and made them eat the parchment, lead seal, *and* silken cord. Thus, they did indeed eat their words—and the idiom was born!

In this chapter, the meaning and origins of many common idioms are explored. As with similes and metaphors, authors and advertisers use these categories of words regularly. The Amelia Bedelia series of books by Peggy Parish relied on the title character Amelia's very literal interpretation of idioms (*hitting the road* . . . with a stick, *drawing the drapes* . . . with paper and pencil, *put the lights out* . . . on the clothesline). More recent authors too, such as Jeff Kinney (2008), use idioms in their writing: in *Diary of a Wimpy Kid*, Greg has *second thoughts* and doesn't want to *spill the beans*. In the world of advertising, financial services firm Deloitte keeps you "ahead of the pack," the GEICO camel walking through the office reminds everyone it's "hump day," and The North Face jackets let you "go the extra mile."

Every language has idioms. Often culturally bound, they can be particularly difficult for ELL students as the sum of the words is different from the individual words (e.g., cats and dogs don't really fall from the sky). Spaniards might say someone's big hairy ears are "like a Volkswagen with doors open," and Russians are not kidding you when they say they're "not hanging noodles on your ears," while the Chinese express an instant attraction between two people as "dry firewood meets a flame" (Bhalla, 2009). We believe your students will enjoy the meanings and stories behind English idioms too, so let's *get down to business* (intense work), put your students *in the driver's seat* (be in charge), and *jump in with both feet* (go all in) for our study of this category of words!

Mary Jo: From the Teacher's Perspective

The origin of *idiom* is from the Greek *idioma* meaning "peculiarity, peculiar phraseology." These phrases are indeed peculiar in their meaning. "Traditionally, idioms are described as fixed expressions, i.e., as phrases or sentences whose figurative meaning is not clear from the literal meaning of their individual constituents" (Abel, 2003, p. 329)—and the dictionary is of little help. If you take them literally, you might miss the intended meaning. The *elephant in the room* (the obvious) might make you feel like you have *egg on your face* (embarrassed) and make you *hold your horses* (wait) because *every dog has its day* (turn in the spotlight). Caillies and Le Sourn-Bissaoui (2008) point out that some idioms are easier to understand than others. For example, *break the ice* is more easily "decomposed" as students can picture ice breaking and apply that to a new context. Conversely, *eat your words* is a "nondecomposable" idiom, or one that cannot be readily defined through reference to the individual words. Researchers found that children as young as five could easily understand decomposable idioms (e.g., *spill the beans*), whereas students needed to be "6 or 7 years old to start to understand nondecomposable idioms" (e.g., *kick the bucket*) (Caillies & Le Sourn-Bissaoui, 2008, p. 709). Interpreting the nondecomposable idiomatic expressions is a mark of having vocabulary that is more syntactically and semantically flexible. Therefore, our students who struggle with comprehension may be puzzled by the less obvious, nondecomposable idioms (Cain et al., 2005). That's where we, as teachers, come in. Drawing attention to idioms in context allows students to more accurately predict and understand their meanings, thus improving comprehension.

Spending time studying idioms also stirs students' curiosity. The vast majority of idioms appear in oral language, but often students will find them in the books they read. Being able to understand an author's intent is important. We must begin the study of idioms when students are in the primary grades, "as failure to understand idioms can interfere with language comprehension in academic settings and extend to the social and vocational settings" (Lundblom & Woods, 2012, p. 203) in the adolescent years. Understanding idioms is regarded as an indication of the development of syntactic and semantic knowledge of vocabulary. Simpson and Mendis's (2003) extensive study found idioms were academically important for a number of pragmatic functions:

- evaluation (*out of whack*)
- description (*run of the mill*)
- paraphrase (*was no mean feat*)
- emphasis (*all but the kitchen sink*)
- collaboration (*put the heat on them*)
- metalanguage (*train of thought*)

While categorizing idioms is the work of linguists, teaching them in context is most useful not only for ELLs but also for native speakers. Many idioms are culturally bound—such as *crying wolf, look before you leap, in the same ballpark*—so clarifying the meanings is easier for students when the pragmatic function is obvious. For instance, a student must understand the idea of a baseball game to comprehend *in the same ballpark* (a similar range or estimate). All ballparks are roughly the same size, so they are estimating two things that are similar in size. *Crying wolf* refers to a fable ("The Boy Who Cried Wolf"), as does *look before you leap* ("The Fox and the Goat"). A study of fables is therefore an excellent connection for exploring idioms.

The English language has more than 25,000 idioms (The Idioms, 2019, para. 2) and there are interesting stories behind each one. Besides the humorous side our language idioms afford, they also can be the beginning place for students to explore etymology, or word origins. "Because they use idioms in their daily speech, students are often interested in learning more about their origins and are often shocked to learn how some phrases came about" (Whitaker, 2008, p. 50). Helping students research is a critical skill that extends beyond learning about idioms. While "curiosity can propel the research they do" (Harrison & Fresch, 2018, p. 29), we can use these investigations as a way to help them learn how to effectively seek information. Many idioms have perfect connections to content studies, so researching them not only gives the history but also teaches the content in new and novel ways. Idiom collections can organize a group of idioms based on a common content theme, such as "ducks" with *She took like a duck to water, sitting ducks, lucky duck,* and *odd duck.* Or, a weather unit might include *raining cats and dogs, under the weather, fair-weather friend, every cloud has a silver lining,* and *save it for a rainy day.* The ideas are endless, and a simple internet search will give you a boatload of ideas! Really, it's a piece of cake!

David: From the Writer's Perspective

As a writer, I must know what the words I use mean so I don't accidentally say the wrong thing. As we discussed in the section on synonyms (Chapter 2), even words that are supposed to mean the same thing seldom mean *exactly* the same thing. But I also need to understand how to use idioms, those common expressions that over time have become part of the language. Where did they come from and what did they originally mean? Idioms can be trickier than single words. Many of them seem to say one thing but mean another. They come from all over the world and back through time, yet have somehow found their way into our daily speech and writing.

For example, in ancient India, worshipers seeking favor from the gods threw little balls of butter at their statues. What does that have to do with you or me? Have you ever used or heard the expression (idiom) to *butter someone up*? We use it when we mean to flatter someone who is in a position to grant us a favor. We hope to get on their good side. How? By buttering them up.

More than two thousand years ago, in the great coliseums in the Roman Empire, gladiators would enter the ring prepared to fight to the death. When one warrior lay wounded on the dirt and his opponent stood over him with his sword ready to strike the last fatal blow, the crowd would signal whether the vanquished gladiator should live or die. A common belief is that, if the crowd liked the way the losing man had fought, they held their thumbs up, meaning for the victor to throw down his sword and let his opponent live. If the crowd had not been pleased, their thumbs down was the signal to kill him. Historians tell us it was really the other way around. Thumbs up was the vote to execute while thumbs down or thumbs wrapped around fists meant the fallen warrior should be spared. Whichever way it was, the thumbs are still with us.

How can we possibly use hand signals for life or death in our language today? If a waiter stops by the table to see how we liked our food, we might give them a cheery smile and *thumbs up* signal. We don't mean we want them to die! We mean we liked what they brought us to eat. If someone asks if we enjoyed the movie, and we didn't, we might say, "Strictly *thumbs down*." But we don't mean anyone should throw down a sword; we mean we don't recommend the movie.

Recognizing Idioms

It helps to recognize an idiom when we see one. Writers use them all the time, but idioms are so common in our speech and writing that we may not always identify them. I find them in books, I hear them on TV, and I catch them in conversations with friends. If I started a list of them, it would soon be a long one that would keep growing. Here is a short list of twenty-three idioms. There are hundreds more. I saw one list that had two thousand idioms on it!

1. out of the blue
2. hadn't cracked a book
3. felt like your goose was cooked
4. in hot water
5. like a bird brain
6. see eye to eye
7. fingers crossed
8. had mixed feelings
9. in the same boat
10. a gray area
11. smart as a whip
12. I'm all ears
13. with flying colors
14. I aced it
15. gotten your act together
16. he drew a blank
17. as cool as a cucumber
18. gave it a shot
19. nailed it
20. as easy as ABC
21. in the bag
22. a piece of cake
23. icing on the cake

When an expression has been in use so long that it has become part of our language, we use it automatically without thinking about it. If we did stop to think, we might agree it doesn't make much sense if we interpret it literally. And there are so many idioms in our language they can bewilder someone who is learning English and trying to make sense of them.

Researching the Origins of Idioms

A challenge that is both entertaining and instructive is to search for the origins of idioms. For example, what did *out of the blue* originally mean? This one isn't too hard. Let's say we have a beautiful day with a blue sky. Suddenly, a fierce thunderstorm strikes—totally unexpected—out of the blue. So, when we say a thing happened "out of the blue," we mean much the same thing. The thing that happened was totally unexpected.

How about *with flying colors*? Colors used to be another name for the flags on ships meant to identify the ship or its country of origin. When a ship sailed into port with its flags (colors) flying, it had returned successfully from its mission. If you pass a test "with flying colors," congratulations—you have returned triumphantly from a great journey at sea! Of course, what we mean these days is that you were successful at something. You were triumphant. You passed the test!

Another benefit of searching for the origins of idioms is that you never know what interesting story-starters you'll find. When I read about a ship's colors, I can imagine a story about a lonely boy waiting for his father to return from the sea, and so spends much of each day on a hill where he will be more likely to spot the flag on his father's ship. How long has the father been gone? How old is the boy? Why is he alone? Is his father okay? Is he really going to make it home? Will the boy go with his father on his next voyage? Will the boy somehow rescue his father? Will his father bring him a present? Just like that, a simple search for the origin of *with flying colors* slips into a bank of ideas to write about.

Using Idioms in Conversation

To see if I could do it, I made up an imaginary conversation that uses all twenty-three of the idioms listed above.

> "Out of the blue, teacher gave us a math test," my friend groaned. "And I hadn't even cracked a book to study."
>
> "Oh no!" I said. "Your goose was cooked!"
>
> "I was in hot water for sure," he agreed. "Sometimes, I think teacher thinks I'm a bird brain. We don't always see eye to eye."
>
> "You must have had your fingers crossed?" I said.
>
> "Let's just say I had mixed feelings," he sighed.
>
> "But wasn't the whole class in the same boat?" I asked.
>
> "Well that's a gray area," my friend said. "Some of the other kids in there are as smart as a whip."
>
> "What happened?" I asked. "I'm all ears."

"I passed the test <u>with flying colors</u>!" he laughed. "I <u>aced it</u>!"

"Wow!" I said. "You must have really <u>gotten your act together</u>."

"For a while, I <u>drew a blank</u> on the first problem," he admitted. "But I stayed <u>cool as a cucumber</u>. I <u>gave it a shot</u> and <u>nailed it</u>. The rest was <u>as easy as ABC</u>. I knew then I had it <u>in the bag</u>."

"A <u>piece of cake</u>," I laughed.

"And getting an A was <u>the icing on the cake</u>," he laughed back.

I did this as an exercise. In real life, I would never cram so many idioms into one short piece of writing. Using too many of any type of words—similes, metaphors, or idioms—can make the writing sound too familiar, too old, too overused. It robs the reader of a more interesting reading experience.

Using Made-Up Idioms in Conversation

For the fun of it, I played with the same make-believe conversation but replaced the real idioms with ones I invented. They don't mean anything. They have no history. I made them up as I went. And they make just as much sense to an ELL student as the real ones.

"<u>Like a runaway cat</u>, teacher gave us a math test," my friend groaned. "And I hadn't even <u>boiled eggs</u> to study."

"Oh no!" I said. "<u>Your belt must have broken</u>!"

"I <u>couldn't see the clouds</u>," he agreed. "Sometimes, I think teacher thinks <u>I'm a T. Rex tail</u>. We <u>don't always sing in the same room</u>."

"You must have <u>blown your balloon</u>?" I said.

"Let's just say <u>I emptied the bucket</u>," he sighed.

"But wasn't the whole class <u>shaggier than a goat</u>?" I asked.

"Well that's <u>for a whale to blow</u>," my friend said. "Some of the other kids in there are <u>as gritty as cereal</u>."

"What happened?" I asked. "I'm <u>falling down</u>."

"I passed the test <u>over two mountains</u>!" he laughed. "I <u>wore the cap</u>!"

"Wow!" I said. "You must have really gotten <u>settled sideways</u>."

"For a while, I <u>considered rocks</u> on the first problem," he admitted. "But I stayed <u>bad as water</u>. I <u>threw it high</u> and <u>peeled the whole orange</u>. The rest was <u>history in the future</u>. I knew then I had it <u>served over rice</u>."

"A <u>spike in the hand</u>," I laughed.

"And getting an A was <u>outwrestling snakes</u>," he laughed back.

Creating Made-Up Origins of Idioms

Now I have a whole new list of made-up idioms. You can imagine the fun I had creating origins for them!

> In 1294, an Irish pub keeper owned a cat that everyone agreed was the orneriest cat anyone had ever seen. That cat's favorite trick was to sneak up on a customer, scratch his ankle, and dash away, leaving the poor victim as surprised as a runaway cat. Today "like a runaway cat" is used to mean, well, out of the blue.

Idiom Lessons

Purpose of Learning

Idioms are used in both speaking and writing. Like other figurative language, such as similes and metaphors, idioms are used to make a message more interesting. Understanding both decomposable and nondecomposable idioms has significant impact on comprehension.

Learnings

To be able to independently recognize the use of an idiom and to assign meaning to it.

Materials
- Idiom Lesson 1—"Defining and Using Idioms" chart (Appendix B, Table B.20), projected
- Idiom Lesson 2—"Idioms, Meanings, and Origins" game cards (Appendix B, Table B.21), photocopied and cut apart to create groups of three (number of matches depends on number of students); you can further support ELL students by copying each set onto different colors of paper, which gives students two ways to match their group
- Idiom Lesson 3—"Idiom Grouping Game" chart and answers (Appendix B, Table B.22 and Table B.23), duplicated for groups of three or four students; these can be cut apart before the lesson, or have each small group cut them apart

---

- Idiom Lesson 4—"Idiom Grouping Game" answers (Appendix B, Table B.23) and "Investigating Idioms" form for students to complete (Appendix B, p. 127)
  - excellent print resources for researching idioms include *In a Pickle and Other Funny Idioms* (Terban, 2007) and *Scholastic Dictionary of Idioms* (Terban, 2008)
  - two student-friendly books available through Kindle Unlimited as free downloads are *The Over-the-Top Histories of Chew the Scenery and Other Idioms* and *The Compelling Histories of Long Arm of the Law and Other Idioms* (Ringstad, 2013a, 2013b)
  - websites to use for researching idiom origins include www.idioms.online (includes short videos that explain the idiom, examples of use, and its origin), www.theidioms.com, https://idioms.thefree dictionary.com, and https://idiomation.wordpress.com/a-z-of-entries
- Idiom Lesson 5—completed form from Lesson 4; example of illustrated idiom (Appendix B, Figure B.1)
- Idiom Lesson 6—David's story for "out of the blue" and "flying colors" (Appendix B, p. 129), Mary Jo's story for "dog days of summer" (Appendix B, p. 130)
- Idiom Lesson 7—chart of idioms and David's story (Appendix B, Table B.24)
- Idiom Lesson 8—chart with David's original story and the version with made-up idioms (Appendix B, Table B.25); "Make Your Own Idioms" handout (Appendix B, p. 133)
- Idiom Lesson 9—David's story for "Origin of 'Like a Runaway Cat'" (Appendix B, p. 134); example story "Origin of 'Ice Cream Days of Summer'" (Appendix B, p. 134); "Make Your Own Idioms" handout from Lesson 8
- Idiom Lesson 10—students' stories about their "made-up" idioms from Lesson 9; "Ice Cream Days of Summer" readers theater script (Appendix B, p. 135)

Idiom Lesson 1

Gather the students to view the "Defining and Using Idioms" chart (Appendix B, Table B.20). Have a student read the first idiom, and ask if anyone has heard of it and might know its meaning. Skip any idioms they do not know. For the ones they know, go back and work together to create a sentence using the idiom. After completing the idiom chart, have students help you write the definition of an idiom. Next, read the histories of each idiom (presented below). Once you have shared the meaning and the history, write sentences together using each idiom.

Apple of my eye

(Favorite or pet.) As far back as the ninth century, the pupil of the eye was considered an important spot of our anatomy. The pupil was apple shaped, and, because it was so vital to life, anything precious (such as loved ones) was called the apple of their eye.

Bury the hatchet

(Settle their differences.) Native Americans would not declare peace between warring tribes until all the warriors had literally buried their hatchets. If this peace was not lasting, the tomahawks were unearthed.

In the nick of time

(Just in time.) Prior to pocket watches and timepieces, times at sporting events were kept track of using a "nick-stick." The nick-stick was used as a way to tally a period of time.

Nest egg

(Saving for the future.) When chickens were domesticated, farmers found that hens were more likely to lay eggs if other eggs were already in the nest. Clever farmers placed a small porcelain egg in the nest. The result was extra eggs that provided a profit. The extra money was set aside and called a "nest egg."

Sleep tight

(Sleep well.) Long ago, mattresses were held up to bed frames through a criss-crossing of ropes. These needed to be tightened occasionally, or the mattress would sag.

Special education teacher Ken Slesarik works one on one with a fifth grader defining idioms.

Idiom Lesson 2

Pass the "Idioms, Meanings, and Origins" game cards (Appendix B, Table B.21) to students, telling them their "buddies" will be an idiom, its meaning, or its origin. You can strategically hand out the origin stories to your more confident readers. Students must find their group of three. Remind them that these are the idioms they learned in Lesson 1. (If students need additional support, you can project the chart from Appendix B, Table B.21, after ten minutes to help finalize the groups.) Have each group share their set after all groups have been formed.

Idiom Lesson 3

Create small groups of three to four students. Distribute the "Idiom Grouping Game" cards from the chart (Appendix B, Table B.22) that have been cut apart. Ask each small group to sort the idioms, putting together phrases that have a common word. Ask them to try to state (or write) the meanings of each idiom. What do they know about the common word (*duck*, *cat*, *horse*) that helps them figure out the meaning? Come together and share their findings. Be sure to discuss the meaning of each idiom in each category. Or, you can pass out the answer chart (Appendix B, Table B.23) and have students self-check their group's sort and discussion. As an extension, have students discuss what the origin might be of each idiom. In Lesson 4, they will be researching these idioms, so have them save their predictions.

Jennifer Harrison's fourth-grade students share their idiom matches.

Idiom Lesson 4

Pass the "Idiom Grouping Game: Answers" chart (Appendix B, Table B.23) to the students. You can choose to have this be an individual, buddy, or small-group inquiry assignment. You can choose other idioms if you wish, or add to this list. Ask students to select one idiom and research its history, using the provided resources. Give them the "Investigating Idioms: Answers" form to record their information (Appendix B, p. 127). Note that the blank space under the "origin" will be used in Lesson 5 for an illustration. Have students share their stories. If they predicted the origin in Lesson 3, were they correct or at least close to the history?

Name:

Idiom: Close but no cigar

Meaning: almost but not quite succseful

Example of idiom in a sentence: She made a good attempt close but no cigar.

Story of the origin of this idiom: The phrase, and it's variat 'nice try, but no cigar', are of U.S orgin and date from the mid-20th century. Fairground stalls gave out cigars as prizes, and this is the most likely source, although there's no definitive evidence to prove that.

"Close but no cigar."

Name:

Idiom:
Sell like hot cakes

Meaning:
A item is being sold quickly

Example of idiom in a sentence:
The tickets for disney world sell like hot cakes.

Story of the origin of this idiom:
The Idiom sell like hot cakes was made because when hot cakes were first sold they were sold very fast.

Name:

Idiom: Turn a Blind Eye

Meaning: Consciously ignore wrongdoing. Ignore something.

Example of idiom in a sentence: She turned a blind eye to the pain in her arm.

Story of the origin of this idiom: The phrase gained popularity after Vice Admiral Nelson used it in the Battle of Copenhagen. The Admiral had been blinded in his right eye. In the Battle of Copenhagen he was ordered stop an attack. But ignored & put the telescope to his blind eye. The Admiral continued to attack, thus turning a blind eye.

Jennifer Harrison's fourth-grade students' idiom research.

Idiom Lesson 5

Return the completed "Investigating Idioms" form from Lesson 4 to the students and ask them to now illustrate the idiom. Ask them to think about an illustration that will convey its meaning. Show the sample "Dog Days of Summer" illustration (Appendix B, Figure B.1) to the students, to clarify the directions. Display their finished illustrations. These sheets could also be available at workstations for students to work on during independent practice sessions.

Idiom Lesson 6

Read aloud David's story about "out of the blue" and "flying colors" (Appendix B, p. 129). You can project this while reading so students can follow along. Or, duplicate the story and pass it out for the students to read. After hearing/reading the story, ask the students to use the idiom they illustrated in Lesson 5 as a prompt for writing a paragraph. Ask them to use the idiom, show its meaning, and provide the history of it. To help, show the example for "dog days of summer" (Appendix B, page 130). These sheets could also be available at workstations for students to work on during independent practice sessions. Have students share their paragraphs and display them for everyone to have time to browse. You might even have students vote for the "cream of the crop" illustration!

Idiom Lesson 7

Read the list of idioms on the left-hand side of the "Idioms–Story" chart (Appendix B, Table B.24) with the students. Work with them to define the ones they know (this is a great formative assessment of their knowledge of idioms that you have not yet reviewed). Highlight the ones they aren't sure of, but don't yet explain them to the students. Then, read David's story (in the right-hand column) all the way through once. Read it a second time, stopping at any idioms students did not originally know. Can they define them from context now? Were they correct on the ones they thought they knew before the lesson?

Idiom Lesson 8

Show the students the two versions of David's story (Appendix B, Table B.25). Remind them the left-hand column is the original story, and that David then had fun making up some idioms and revised his story to include these. Read the story in the right-hand column. Which ones did they like the best? Which ones made them laugh? Which ones could they picture?

Next, give the students the "Make Your Own Idioms" handout (Appendix B, p. 133), asking them to fill in the blanks with their own ideas. Show how *dog days of summer* was changed to *ice cream days of summer*. Have them share their new idioms when they are finished.

Idiom Lesson 9

Show the students David's story "Origin of 'Like a Runaway Cat'" (Appendix B, p. 134). Remind them that he made up this idiom to replace "out of the blue" when he rewrote his story (see Lesson 8). Show the students the "ice cream days of summer" story as another example. Return the "Make Your Own Idioms" handouts to students. Ask them to make up their own origin of one or more of the idioms. This lesson can extend into writing time or any other independent practice time. Have students share their stories.

Idiom Lesson 10

Remind students that, on the "Make Your Own Idioms" handout, *ice cream days of summer* was an example of a made-up idiom. Then, show them the story from Lesson 9 again, "Origin of 'Ice Cream Days of Summer.'" Next, tell students they will be in small groups to create a readers theater script of one of their member's made-up idiom stories. Use the "Ice Cream Days of Summer" script (Appendix B, p. 135) as an example. Hand students the script to show how they might think about dramatizing their own stories. Ask three students to read the parts (Narrator, Nero Claudis Caesar, and Benjerry). Show how the story was divided up and speakers added to create the readers theater.

Organize students into small groups. Ask them to select one group member's story from Lesson 9 to dramatize. Give students time to organize their presentations. Have groups perform their readers theater.

Kristi Prince's fourth graders play an idiom matching game.

Independent Practice: Empowering Vocabulary Lessons

1. Put the game cards from Lesson 2 at a workstation and have students play a memory matching game with them.

2. Place the chart with idioms (Appendix B, p. 125) at a workstation or make it available during independent practice times. Provide the resources used in Lesson 4. Have students find the origin of one of the idioms listed.

3. Using the same list as above, ask students to illustrate one of the idioms listed.

4. Allow small groups of students to select real stories about idioms and create readers theater scripts to perform.

Let It Rain

These idiom exercises bring the idea of figurative language to the attention of your students. When they listen, they will perk up and notice idioms you have discussed. When they read, they will be more aware of an author's use of figurative language to enrich their writing. When students write, they may find ways to use idioms to make their compositions more colorful. One final idea for the classroom is to have an "Afternoon Idiom Challenge," by showing an idiom each day. Project it on a screen or write it on a chart that students can see as they enter the room from lunch or a special class. Suggest they think about the meaning until everyone settles in. Then, a quick conversation about it will bring the meaning to clarity. Here are a few to get you started:

- all ears
- bark up the wrong tree
- crack a book
- curiosity killed the cat
- down to the wire
- eager beaver
- get cold feet
- having second thoughts
- in hot water
- slipped my mind

As meaning is best conveyed in context, an extension of the Afternoon Idiom Challenge is to ask students to compose a paragraph using the idiom of the day. What story could include *beat around the bush* or *throw a curve*? Post these for students to share and enjoy. Or, continue the inquiry approach by allowing a few students each day to research and present the history of an idiom. It's *all over but the shouting*!

5

Making Our Language More Colorful: Shades of Meaning and Word Origins

The English language is nobody's special property. It is the property of the imagination: it is the property of the language itself.

—*Sir Derek Walcott*

Throughout this book, we have approached enriching vocabulary by engaging students in active, hands-on strategies. We look to wordplay as an essential element of learning vocabulary. Explicit instruction to help students know a wide range of words is needed for success in reading, writing, and speaking. We know there is a strong correlation between vocabulary knowledge and reading comprehension. Developing an extensive meaning vocabulary (words students understand and can readily use) is important in order to give all students access to texts. Authors often use multiple ways to describe the same content, so understanding shades of meaning taps directly into improved comprehension.

With an emphasis on active engagement, all students can participate in learning new words. In learning vocabulary, we must not forget the usefulness of teaching how context clues can help clarify meanings. For instance, in using the more formal word *meteorologist* (students will most likely be familiar with *weatherperson*), an author might use one of four types of context clues:

1. definition—Sam is a *meteorologist*, a person who studies the weather.

2. synonym or restatement—Sam is a *meteorologist*, or a weatherman.

3. antonym or contrast—Sam is a *meteorologist*. Unlike the sportscaster, he reports the weather.

4. inference—Sam is just like Al Roker on the *Today* show; he's a *meteorologist*!

Our goal is to give students independent strategies for reading, writing, and speaking to deepen their knowledge of words.

In this chapter, we examine two playful ways to increase students' vocabulary power. First, David takes apart a paragraph to examine *shades of meaning*. Second, we explore *word origins* as a way to deepen knowledge about words, engage students in storytelling (a tried-and-true activity students enjoy), and spark interest in the English language. We strive for our students to know a word well, and to be able to recall and properly use it. A sometimes-problematic error students make when trying to "jazz" up their writing is to replace a "less exciting" word with one for which they do not have decontextualized knowledge. We cannot always substitute Word A for Word B. A classic episode of the television show *Friends* ("The One Where Rachel's Sister Babysits") demonstrates the folly in using a thesaurus without considering context. In Joey's letter of reference about his friends, he writes, "They're humid prepossessing homo sapiens with full-sized aortic pumps" (having used a thesaurus to make the original sentence "They're warm, nice people with big hearts" sound more impressive)! Perhaps he needed different "shades" of meaning to describe his friends. We want our students to attain precision, or the ability to correctly use words in multiple contexts. This high-order thinking process is key to developing a wide and deep understanding of vocabulary.

Shades of Meaning

Mary Jo: From the Teacher's Perspective

Shades of meaning strategies not only enrich our writing, but also deepen an understanding of words. However, synonymous words can have shades of meaning that do or do not work in certain situations. For instance, *funny* could be replaced by *hilarious* when describing a comedian, but that same replacement would sound odd when talking about how the milk smells. Students must be encouraged to evaluate the context for the accuracy of the use of words. Drawing attention to how an author provides a shade of meaning can help students learn independent reading strategies.

Blachowicz and Fisher (2004) suggest having students place shades-of-meaning words along a continuum to show gradation. One strong visual approach for teaching this is to use paint chips from a hardware or paint store. One word—for example, *mad*—is placed at one end, with the palest color; next is *angry*, then *irate*, and finally *furious* is at the other end, where the color is deeper and more intense. The "intensity" of the words is visualized through the deepening shades of paint colors.

Shades of meaning is using words with similar meaning, but with more "punch." We can substitute colorful words that would fall at the same gradient as a less powerful word. Table 5.1 presents some examples.

TABLE 5.1. Example Shades of Meaning Words

asked	→	requested	→	demanded
inquired	→	summoned	→	mandated

Working together to examine a paragraph that has potential for substituting shades of meaning is a good way to start students thinking about how this applies to their writing. Revision of writing often needs consideration for shades of meaning: "How can I better describe the setting, character, or action?" Looking back at what students have learned about figurative language (similes, metaphors, idioms) gives yet another way to intensify the writing. David offers an example in the next section.

David: From the Writer's Perspective

Some people tell a better story than others. Some books are more fun to read than others. Some people are more interesting to listen to than others. Why is that? Having and using a good vocabulary isn't the whole answer, but it's a vital part of it. This book is about ways to increase students' vocabulary but also to show them how to choose the best words in the right places at the right time.

Using similes, metaphors, nyms, and idioms comes naturally with time and practice. The better students understand these elements of our language, the sooner they will learn how to apply them in their own speaking and writing. To provide an example of how, by increasing students' vocabulary, we improve their opportunities to communicate on a higher level, let's write a description of a witch flying through a terrible storm. It's nighttime but she's not afraid. She's laughing.

> A witch was flying through a terrible storm. It was nighttime. She wasn't afraid. She was laughing.

Not very exciting is it? What does it need? More description. More action. Better vocabulary! What kind of clouds? Is there any lightning? What does it look like when a witch flies through a nighttime storm? Is it noisy up there? What about thunder? How do we know the witch is having fun? Can we hear her laughing? Does the witch have a name?

With those questions in mind, let's try it again.

> Huge storm clouds filled the sky. When lightning flashed, you could see a witch flying among the clouds. You could hear her laughing above the sound of thunder. Far below, everything was quiet. But, up high, the storm was howling. It was a good night for Sally the witch to go flying. She felt reckless. She yelled happily as she flew.

Better. Much better! Now we know more about the way the storm looks and sounds. We know about the witch and even her name. What else do we need to bring our narrative to life? By putting the lessons in this book to use, we might:

- replace "Huge storm clouds" with a *metaphor*: "Clouds were volcanoes"
- replace "filled" with a stronger *synonym*: "erupting"
- replace "flashed" with a stronger *synonym*: "crackled"
- give lightning a *metaphor*: "blue-white tongue"
- replace "witch flying" with more action words and a *simile*: "darting form swooped and glided like a bony black bird"
- replace "laughing" with stronger *synonym*: "cackling"
- provide details of how Sally is having fun: "Double loop. Slow roll. Graceful dive"
- replace "storm" with a surprising *metaphor*: "delicious brew"
- replace "howling" with a more related *synonym*: "brewing"
- use a *metaphor* for clouds: "mountains"
- give Sally a more appropriate witch name: "Xxxxlntz"
- show how "reckless" Sally was with an *idiom*: "throwing caution to the wind"
- replace "yelled happily" with *synonyms*: "shrieked with joy"
- conclude with a witchy idiom: "happier than a toad in a mud puddle."

We've now transformed our original narrative:

> A witch was flying through a terrible storm. It was nighttime. She wasn't afraid. She was laughing.

to this:

> Clouds were volcanoes erupting in the night. A blue-white tongue of lightning crackled across the sky. Cackling merrily, a darting form swooped and glided like a bony, black bird. A double loop. A slow roll. A graceful dive. Shrill laughter rang out above rumbling thunder. Thirty thousand feet below, the world was sleeping. Up here, a delicious brew was boiling. A perfect night for a witch to play tag with lightning and slide down cloud mountains. Xxxxlntz, or "Sally" as she was sometimes called, loved every thump and crash of it. Throwing caution to the wind, she shrieked with joy, happier than a toad in a mud puddle. (Adapted from Graham, 1976, p. 48)

Shades of Meaning Lessons

Purpose of Learning

Authors often use multiple ways to describe the same content, so understanding shades of meaning taps directly into improved comprehension. Shades of meaning can improve writing and provide a more powerful engagement for our readers.

Learnings

To be able to discern shades of meaning and apply them independently when writing.

Materials
- Shades of Meaning Lesson 1—David's original and revised witch narratives, projected or photocopied (Appendix B, p. 136); David's second revised witch narrative, projected or photocopied (Appendix B, p. 136); photocopied "Revised Narrative" handout, for buddies to work on together (Appendix B, p. 138)

- Shades of Meaning Lesson 2—"The Fox & the Grapes" story, for large-group viewing (Appendix B, p. 139), "The Ant & the Dove," photo-copied for individual use (Appendix B, p. 139)
- Shades of Meaning Lesson 3— "Shades of Meaning Matching Game" word cards, photocopied and cut apart (one per student) (Appendix B, Table B.26); "Shades of Meaning Matching Game" handout, to complete with buddy (Appendix B, p. 141)
- Shades of Meaning Lesson 4—"Word Order" handout (Appendix B, Table B.27); scissors

Shades of Meaning Lesson 1

Read the following aloud to the students, telling them it is a story from David:

> Some people tell a better story than others. Some books are more fun to read than others. Some people are more interesting to listen to than others. Why is that? Having and using a good vocabulary isn't the whole answer, but it's a vital part of it. Using similes, metaphors, nyms, and idioms comes naturally with time and practice. Here's an example of how we can communicate on a higher level. Let's write a description of a witch flying through a terrible storm. It's nighttime but she's not afraid. She's laughing.

Next, show students the original witch narrative (Appendix B, p. 136). Tell them David thought it was unimaginative, so he wanted to fix it. Show the revised witch narrative (Appendix B, p. 136). Talk about how David expanded the story by adding more details.

After that, show David's second revision of the narrative (Appendix B, p. 136) and the list he provided of the changes he made. Point out how he used what we have been learning all along in the previous lessons.

Finally, pair students up and provide the "Revised Narrative" handout (Appendix B, p. 138) for them to work on.

> **I rode the bus to school. It was Tuesday. We will have gym** ~~Autumn~~
>
> **today. It might rain.** ~~and Cheyanne~~

I rode the dredful bus to school. It looks and feels like a prison. The bus is as yellow as a lemon. It's Tuesday and I don't want to go to school because we have gym. My gym teacher is the Wicked Witch of the West. Also, the school play is today. I have the lead role and everyone says "break a leg!" I bet they can see the future. My teacher said we can have added recess but it might rain today. Either way, I can go home and relax.

Fourth graders Autumn and Cheyanne revise a story.

Shades of Meaning Lesson 2

Project the "The Fox & the Grapes" story (Appendix B, p. 139). (The original text was sourced from the Library of Congress's open-access Aesop for Children website: www.read.gov/aesop/005.html. There are also short animations illustrating the stories here.)

Read the entire paragraph together. Then, ask students to look at the underlined words. Can they suggest a more powerful word, idiom, or metaphor in its place? Remind them their choice still has to make sense in the context of the story. Possible alternative words are listed in Table 5.2.

TABLE 5.2. "The Fox & the Grapes": Shades of Meaning Words

burst: explode, rupture, gush, erupt	hung: dangled, drooped, sagged	high: lofty, soaring, tiptop, tall	jumped: vaulted, leaped, bound
running: galloping, sprinting, dashing	sat: slouched, squatted, plopped, slumped	looked at: gazed up at, studied, eyed	walked: stomped, marched

Be sure to discuss the meaning of Aesop's moral to this story. Ask students to help you craft a definition for *shades of meaning*.

After doing this together, give buddies a copy of "The Ant & the Dove" (Appendix B, p. 139). Tell them to read the entire fable first. Then, ask them to substitute an idiom, simile, or metaphor in place of each underlined word. Gather as a whole group and have buddies share their responses (this is also a great formative assessment of your students' vocabulary knowledge). Ask them if they noticed the simile (*like a shipwrecked sailor*)! Discuss Aesop's moral.

Shades of Meaning Lesson 3

Remind students of the *shades of meaning* definition crafted in Lesson 1. Pass the "Shades of Meaning Matching Game" word cards (Appendix B, Table B.26) out to students and have them find their buddy with a similar meaning. You can strategically pass out the cards to be sure students have success based on the difficulty of the word. Pass out a copy of the "Shades of Meaning Matching Game" handout (Appendix B, p. 141) to each pair of students. Ask the pair to follow the directions. Post these for all students to see. Suggest they browse these sets for ideas on word choice and shades of meaning when independently writing.

Shades of Meaning Lesson 4

Group students in pairs. Distribute the "Word Order" handout to them (Appendix B, Table B.27). Have students cut apart each "column" of word cards and ask them to place them in the order of least powerful to most powerful (see Table 5.3). (Roam the room during this time to listen in on conversations of how students justify the order, the meanings, etc.) When everyone is done, share, compare, and discuss! If there's time, ask students to suggest another set of words. You could suggest a word to get them started, such as *big*, and then let them offer ideas.

TABLE 5.3. Word Order: Less Powerful–More Powerful

good	→	excellent	→	awesome
nibble	→	eat	→	devour
hard	→	difficult	→	challenging
call	→	yell	→	scream

Independent Practice: Empowering Vocabulary Lessons

1. Provide the Shades of Meaning Matching Game handout (Appendix B, p. 141) at a workstation. You may want to provide dictionaries and thesauri for resources.

2. Provide a workstation where students can get online for the Aesop's fables used in Lesson 1 (www.read.gov/aesop/001.html). Have students choose another fable and select words to exchange to show shades of meaning.

Word Origins

Mary Jo: From the Teacher's Perspective

As with the histories of idioms, delving into word origins can engage students in new and exciting ways. Words can be drawn from across the curriculum. While digging into the etymologies, or word histories, you are also teaching content. For instance, *twelve* is from the Old English meaning "two left" . . . past ten (we count with ten fingers, so, with twelve, have "two left"; *eleven* means "one left"). *Deadline* has roots in the US Civil War when "stockades" for prisoners were made by drawing lines in the dirt. If a prisoner crossed the line, they were shot (it was a *dead*line). In Chapter 2, we explored the origins of eponyms, or words from people's names. Content areas abound with them. For example:

-   science: *Fahrenheit, Celsius, volt, watt*
-   social studies: *America, atlas, boycott, Braille, Morse code*
-   everyday life: *sandwich, derrick, leotard, Ferris wheel, graham cracker, Buffalo wings*

Curious about these stories? Go to the online etymology dictionary www.etymonline.com to discover their origins and to find your own cross-curricular stories that students will love to repeat.

These stories tap into the natural human interest in storytelling, are entertaining, and often explain the spelling of words. *Album, albatross, albumin,* and *albino* all come from *albus,* meaning "white." Ties to literature can often be found, such as J. K. Rowling's Albus Dumbledore, who has a white beard . . . and *Dumbledore* is an archaic word for "bumblebee" (he is always humming to himself as he walks around). E. B. White named the family in *Charlotte's Web* the Arables, which means "farmable." Even origins of first names give us insights into the works of authors: *Charlotte* means "little woman" and *Wilbur* means "wild boar." Looking up name origins can be a fun first look at etymologies. Baby name books and websites such as www.behindthename.com offer resources for this activity. Students can find their name and retell the story of the origin (or create a story, if one does not exist).

Storytelling has a long history as a way to pass knowledge to the next generation. Bruner (2002) claims storytelling is universal. It undoubtedly enhances language skills and develops vocabulary and syntax. Storytelling can work across the curriculum too. It can take vocabulary learning out of the memorization model and into "making memories" about words. Students are not passive recipients, but, rather, actively engaged and likely to better remember stories about words. Indeed, "teachers discovered that children could easily recall whatever historical or scientific facts they learned through story" (National Council of Teachers of English, 1992, para. 2); in particular, research points to the assistance "story" gives to ELL students in vocabulary gains. Having students actively engaged in hearing (and telling) stories about words makes learning memorable.

Telling the story of the word *silhouette* is a good example of this. Étienne de Silhouette was a French finance minister during the mid-1700s. While it was tradition for aristocrats to have their children's portrait done, Silhouette, being a man of finance, did not want to spend the money for an oil painting. So he asked the artist to simply outline his children's features. (This is one explanation—there are others.) Art, history, and economics all merge in this one story! And, speaking of the class system, many of our multiple words that mean the same thing are due to invasions, the plague, and a large peasant population. Until the Norman conquests of England in 1066, the peasants spoke an Anglo-Saxon/Germanic-based language. The aristocracy spoke French (which is Latin based). Thus, two complete languages joined, and "English" was born. Consequently, a poor farmer raised *chickens* (Germanic roots), but a rich aristocrat ate *poultry* (French roots). The noble class would *perspire* (French) or *exude* (Latin), but the peasants would *sweat* (Germanic). These words also return us to the shades of meaning discussed earlier in this chapter. Saying someone was having *escargot* for dinner sounds much tastier than saying they were having *snails*! Once you start sharing these stories with students, they sit up and notice them in their own reading. You might begin to hear, "I wonder where _____ came from?"

Word Origin Lessons

Purpose of Learning

Word origins often provide explanations of why words are spelled as they are. The study of word origins stirs curiosity in students and makes words memorable. It is a word study technique that can cross the curriculum.

Learnings

Exploration of word origins to expand knowledge of words, to see relationships with other words, and to make words and their definitions memorable (and retrievable).

Materials

- Word Origin Lesson 1—"I've Got a Secret" chart (Appendix B, Table B.28); "Word Origins" story sheet, one per student or pairs of students (Appendix B, Table B.29)

- Word Origin Lesson 2—"Word–Origin–Definition Partner Matching Game" cards sets, cut apart (Appendix B, Table B.30 and Table B.31); each student or pair of students should have one of the three cards that make a set; to differentiate this activity, print each column on different colors of paper (e.g., words on green, origins on yellow, definitions on blue), which will assist the students as they make their groups

- Word Origin Lesson 3—Fairy Tale Partner Matching cards, cut apart (Appendix B, Table B.32); projectable example tree (Appendix B, Figure B.2); six copies of word web trees (Appendix B, Figure B.3), enlarged on chart paper; post on walls around the room or spread out on tabletops

---

Susan Hutchens prepares word origin matching cards of different colors to support her ELL students.

Word Origin Lesson 1

Display the "I've Got a Secret" chart with multiple-choice options for a word and its origin (Appendix B, p. 144). With each word, ask students to turn and talk to their "elbow buddy." Which origin is correct? Ask them about their guesses and then provide the correct answer for each (tulip–*tulbend*; window–"wind eye"; canoe–"hollow log"; hurricane–*huraca'n*; globe–*globus*; comet–*kometes*). After going through all six words, pass out the "Word Origins" story sheet (Appendix B, p. 144). Have students take turns reading them aloud. What surprises them?

Word Origin Lesson 2

Give each student or pair of students one card from the "Word–Origin–Definition Partner Matching Game" (Appendix B, p. 146). You can strategically hand out cards based on your students' reading levels. You might support challenged or ELL students by giving them the word cards, while more accomplished readers could have the origin cards. The definition cards should be handed to students comfortable reading most texts. Or, if you have printed the cards using three different colors, tell the students each group will have only one of each color. Once the cards are passed out, ask students to find their set of three: (1) a word, (2) its definition, and (3) its origin. When all sets are made, have students read aloud the three cards.

Word Origin Lesson 3

Project the example word web tree (Appendix B, Figure B.2). Show students the root of the tree and that the words in the branches are related to it. Note that all the words have to do with *star*. Read aloud the explanations of each word, showing the connection to *aster* or "star."

Next, use Fairy Tale Partner Matching Cards as an organizer for creating small groups (Appendix B, p. 147). Once the groups are together, have each group stand by one tree (Appendix B, Figure B.3; six copies, enlarged on chart paper). Explain that they are to write words in the branches related in meaning to their root. Let each small group get started on their tree, then, after five minutes, ask the groups to move to the next tree on their right. Ask them to write any words in the branches they can think of that are not already there. After five minutes, ask them to move again. Repeat until each group has visited each tree. Gather the group in front of each tree to discuss the words and their meanings. Encourage students to explain the words, as was done with the *aster* tree example. For example, if they wrote *biography*, the explanation would be *bio* (life) and *graph* (to write)—so a *biography* would be the writing about one's life.

Possible related words for the six trees could include:

1. *graph* (to write)—autograph, graphic, graphite, geography, photograph, biography
2. *sign* (to mark)—signature, signal, design, signify, significant
3. *tract* (to pull or drag)—subtract, traction, extract, detract, tractor, attract
4. *cent* (hundred)—century, cent, centipede, centennial, centigrade
5. *port* (to carry)—import, deport, export, transport, report, portfolio, support, portable
6. *meter* (measure)—metric, thermometer, speedometer, perimeter, centimeter, odometer

Leave these on display for students to add to during the week (see also the "Empowering Vocabulary" lesson below).

Independent Practice: Empowering Vocabulary Lessons

1. Leave the independent inquiry "Word Origins" handout (Appendix B, p. 150) at a workstation, or distribute it during independent work time. Have students complete the handout.

2. Place the cards used in Lesson 2 at a workstation for students to use as a memory matching game.

3. Leave the trees made in Lesson 3 on display. Tell students to add a word whenever they find one that fits with that root. Content glossaries are good resources for additional words. Extend the learning by adding additional blank trees with different roots, such as *bio*–life; *auto*–self; *vis* or *vid*–to see; or *photo*–light.

Closing This Chapter and Our Book

Learning about shades of meaning and word origins empowers students' vocabulary by helping them see relationships among words. This deeper understanding of how words are related guides them toward more rewarding reading and imaginative writing. When we awaken student interest in shades of meaning and the origin of words, we also stir curiosity about language itself that leads to self-motivated research with "sticking power," as students go on to make further discoveries.

Now, as promised in Chapter 1, we finish this book with words of wisdom from some of today's most gifted authors of children's literature. Like all good magicians, the tricks of their trade are often hard to spot. Yet their stories are visible proof of what happens when we understand and put to work similes, metaphors, synonyms, shades of meaning, and related words. Some of these wonderful wordsmiths have worked at their trade so long they are hardly aware of how they put these elements of good writing together. You and your students will find their responses as fascinating and illuminating as we did. And it turns out they all want the same thing we do—to empower students' vocabulary!

Making Their Writing Come Alive: Inside Tips from Popular Children's Authors

The best writing is rewriting.

—*E. B. White*

As we bring our book to a close, we thought we should write a summary of what we've presented. After all is said and done (we write, *idiomatically.* . .), in what ways should young writers benefit? How is all this supposed to come together to make students (or anyone else) better readers and writers? Then we had a brainstorm (*metaphorically.* . .). Instead of writing our own version of that answer, why not ask a number of America's favorite children's poets and authors to talk about their own writing?

"Brilliant," David said, stroking his chin.

"Brilliant," Mary Jo hmmed professorially.

So out went invitations to several prominent writers, asking for their help. We told them what our book is about and gave them an example from it to help them set their sights. The rest was up to them. It is with pleasure that we present their wonderful responses in this concluding chapter.

We think you will enjoy what our guest authors have to say as much as we did. No two reflections are the same. Some of our most successful authors admit to rarely if ever sitting down and *intentionally* searching for just the right idiom, the most robust metaphor, or the perfect synonym to make their work memorable. Yet their work sparkles with diamonds they embed in their sentences that keep readers turning pages looking for more. Other great writers give us specific examples of how they mold and shape their work—and how your students can too. You'll see that everyone gets there by a different path, but everyone gets there. Responses are not arranged in a particular order. This group of experts shows how our English language can be used to paint an endless array of pictures. And THAT is what this book is all about—helping students become better and better at painting word pictures of their own.

"The Magic of Metaphors!" by Charles Ghigna

Clouds are popcorn. Lakes are mirrors. Snowflakes are butterflies dressed all in white. Shadows are best friends who come out at night. Those are metaphors. Metaphors are comparisons. Thinking up metaphors is fun. It's magic! In fact, the phrase "metaphors are magic" is a metaphor!

When you use a metaphor to develop an idea or scene throughout a poem or story, it is called an extended metaphor. I often like to use extended metaphors to hold the interest of my readers as they make their way into and through my poems. Like a good tour guide, an extended metaphor provides the reader with a little path to "show, rather than tell," what the journey is all about.

Along the way, I like to add images that relate to the extended metaphor. Those added images help provide interest to the path and clarity to the journey, much like one who experiences the trees, flowers, birds, bees, and butterflies along their stroll through a path in the woods.

Here are three poems in which I used an extended metaphor. The first poem is written in first person point of view ("we"), and uses an extended metaphor to compare the writing of a poem to the building of a house. The second poem is written in second person point of view ("you"), and uses an extended metaphor to compare a poem to a path. The third poem is a free verse poem (no rhymes) written in third person point of view ("they"), and uses an extended metaphor to compare cars covered in snow to birthday cakes with streetlights for candles, and the North Wind personified as the person who comes to make a wish and blow out the candles.

How to Build a Poem

Let's build a poem
made of rhyme
with words like ladders
we can climb,
with words that like
to take their time,

words that hammer,
words that nail,
words that saw,

words that sail,
words that whisper,
words that wail,

words that open
window   door,
words that sing,
words that soar,
words that leave us
wanting more.

A Poem Is a Little Path

A poem is a little path
That leads you through the trees.
It takes you to the cliffs and shores,
To anywhere you please.

Follow it and trust your way
With mind and heart as one,
And when the journey's over,
You'll find you've just begun.

Snowfall in the City

Covered in creamy
birthday-cake frosting,
the parked cars
huddle beneath
their streetlamp candles
waiting for the North Wind
to come make its wish
for morning.

Now you try it! What subject would you like to write about? What metaphor (comparison) will you choose? Sometimes, it's fun to compare abstract things to real things, such as comparing hope (abstract) to a kite (concrete image). Look around. Metaphors are everywhere! Maybe you can find one to compare to painting a picture, planting a garden, playing a game. Have fun finding metaphors and using your imagination to turn them into magic.

What's a Meadow For?

My teacher asked, "May I implore,
What is a metaphor?"

I thought of fields of butterflies
And daffodils and sunny skies.
My answer caught her by surprise:

A meadow's for the cows to graze,
A place I spend my lazy days,
Where spiders spin their magic maze
And bumble bees perform ballets.

My teacher smiled and smiled some more.
"Now that's an answer I adore.
A meadow's for a metaphor!"

"A Personal Story" by Jane Yolen

As a writer, I love words wholeheartedly. We remember where some of them came from even into our old age. (Or "dotage" which is an old-fashioned word for old age, and a lot prettier.)

I remember learning the word "soporific" which means something that makes you sleepy in Beatrix Potter's picture book *The Tale of the Flopsy Bunnies* in which the rabbits believe that lettuce is soporific.

But language changes as new people join the conversation. Usage changes. And sometimes writers MAKE NEW WORDS UP.

Poets and song writers do this a lot. Take the song from the Disney movie *Mary Poppins* "Supercalifragilisticexpialidocious": it has become a fun word in the English language.

Teens make up words and phrases all the time. "Throwing shade."

Babies do, too.

Science, history journalists add new words. As do immigrants speaking another language.

As does a misspelled presidential tweet.

Here's a personal story about a new word I invented and used in a book.

Our family rented a cabin in Vermont for a ski trip one year when our children were fairly young. But I was working on a picture book called *Nocturne* so while my husband David took our kids skiing I stayed behind, trying to work on finishing the book. So I sat there in the little ski cottage (this was before computers and the internet) with two different dictionaries and a small encyclopedia I'd brought along. And a children's nonfiction book about the moon. I needed to solve a few things in the manuscript and all but one came easily. However, here was a line when the boy—who has gone outside in the night with his mother—looks up at the moon sailing above them like a balloon. I needed a word to highlight it. A munchy word. Something surprising. Ballooning seemed too simple.

He was out in the night, which was not quiet at all, and it was chittering and singing around him.

I read about the moon in the moon book and encyclopedia. They were no help.

Looked up moon synonyms in the dictionary, nada.

Looked up noise—the word "hullaballoo" was almost right but not quite.

I walked outside in the snow, wandered a bit down the road, because taking a walk often helps me think about things.

And, as I was coming back, I thought about the moon ballooning and the hullabaloo in the evening and came up with a made-up word: "Hullabalooning!"

It was perfect!

And when David and the kids returned, I greeted them doing a bit of hullabalooning myself. None of them blanched. I no longer surprised them. Except in a good way.

"Poetry Fridays" by Janet Wong

My colleague Sylvia Vardell and I have created the Poetry Friday Anthology series, which features more than seven hundred poems by one hundred fifty poets. We think Fridays are perfect for sharing poetry—we love the idea of sharing poems as a treat for the end of the week—but of course we want everyone to share poems all week long, too. I wrote a poem "Poetry Fridays," which appears in *GREAT Morning! Poems for School Leaders to Read Aloud*, with these thoughts in mind (Wong, 2018, p. 17).

I could simply rearrange these thoughts into a poem, splitting the sentences into poem lines, as follows:

Fridays are perfect
for sharing poetry.
We love the idea
of sharing poems
as a treat
for the end
of the week.
But of course
we want everyone
to share poems
all week long, too.

But by using some more interesting word choices—choices inspired and driven by rhyme, repetition, rhythm, alliteration, and a bit of metaphor—here's what I created instead:

Poetry Fridays
by Janet Wong

Poetry Mondays make us mindful,
calm us down, help us see.

Poetry Tuesdays tell our stories.
Let's write poems . . . starring *me*!

Wednesdays are for poems and art.
Words plus pictures make us smart.

On Poetry Thursdays we do STEM.
Poet? Scientist? We're both of them!

But of all the days, Friday is king.
Poetry Fridays are EVERYTHING!

My word choices in this poem are simple. The hardest words are "mindful" and the acronym "STEM" and I help readers understand those words with the lines that follow each of them. Sometimes, I get dazzled by "fancy words"— especially when I'm trying to rhyme—and those fancy words can pull me away from my meaning. So, most of the time, I try to write as simply as I can. Simple words can still be powerful. The trick is asking yourself, as you are re-reading your work and revising, "Does this really say what I meant to say?"

"Mr. King Is Not Always Right" by Larry Dane Brimner

Any word you have to hunt for in a thesaurus is the wrong word. There are no exceptions to this rule.

—*Stephen King*

The problem with the advice above is that Stephen King doesn't have my editor. It is human nature for people, even people with college-educated vocabularies, to use words that are familiar and comfortable. A person's vocabulary is almost like a fingerprint, and, because of this, it can lead to the repetitious use of particular words or phrases. Here's what I mean: in one middle-grade book, I'd written about a mob, meaning a large group of angry, violent people. The mob did this. The mob did that. I hadn't realized I'd used the word *mob* three or four or perhaps five times on the page until my editor asked if there was some other word I might use instead to provide some variety for the reader. A quick look through the thesaurus I kept at the edge of my desk—I use an online thesaurus now—provided the following alternatives, or synonyms: crowd, horde, throng, gang, rabble-rousers, and group of thugs. I carefully picked a few that worked within the passage I'd written, and the change provided a more lively reading experience for the reader and one that wasn't repetitious.

Think about it. An old man walked down the street. He walked up the steps. He walked into his house. He walked into his kitchen and sat down to dinner. It's pretty ho–hum, isn't it? A few well-chosen synonyms could enliven the passage and even provide a few clues to his mood at the same time.

My response to Mr. King is no, sometimes a thesaurus can be helpful, and can save the writer from putting the audience to sleep.

"Repeating Sounds in Poetry" by Kenn Nesbitt

When a poet writes a poem, they often will think of many ways to write each line. Even after they choose the words they feel best express what they are trying to say, they may go back and rewrite it more than once. Change a word here, a phrase there, until they can find no way to improve what they have written.

Some writers focus on using metaphors or similes to make their writing more compelling. Or they choose more interesting synonyms or onomatopoeias.

When I write a poem, I prefer to focus on the repetitions of sounds; the way that repeating certain sounds can make reading a poem more enjoyable and almost musical. This includes not just rhymes and rhythm, but also alliterations and something known as *assonance*.

A rhyme is when words end with the same sounds. When you read a rhyming poem the rhymes are often the first thing you notice. But, if you look closely, you may notice the poet repeating other sounds as well.

Alliteration is when words have the same consonant *sound* (not necessarily the same letter) at the beginnings of nearby words. For example, "cats and kittens" is an alliteration because both words start with a "k" sound, even though *cats* starts with the letter "c." On the other hand, "golf and gymnastics" is not an alliteration. Even though both words start with the same letter, the "g" in "golf" is a hard "g," while the "g" in "gymnastics" is soft and pronounced like a "j."

But my favorite sound repetition of all is assonance. Assonance is when you repeat the vowel sounds of nearby words. For example, "light a fire" repeats the long "i" vowel sound in the words "light" and "fire." Similarly, "dump truck" repeats the short "u" vowel sound and "go slow" repeats the long "o" vowel sounds.

When I write and I think of different ways to phrase a line, I listen for the sounds of the rhymes, the alliterations, and the assonance. To show you how this works in practice, here are a few lines from my poem "My Puppy Punched Me in the Eye" from my book *My Hippo Has the Hiccups*.

> My puppy punched me in the eye.
> My rabbit whacked my ear.
> My ferret gave a frightful cry
> and roundhouse kicked my rear.

At first glance, you may notice that "eye" rhymes with "cry" and "ear" rhymes with "rear."

If you look a little closer, you might notice several alliterations. "Puppy" and "punched" both start with a "p" sound. "Ferret" and "frightful" both begin with an "f" sound. And "roundhouse" and *rear* have the same beginning "r" sound.

And, if you look even closer, you might notice a couple of places where I repeated vowel sounds: "puppy" and "punched" both have a short "u" sound and "rabbit" and "whacked" both have a short "a" sound. I love the way the assonance makes these lines sound.

Let's look at a few more lines.

> My lizard flipped me upside down.
> My kitten kicked my head.
> My hamster slammed me to the ground
> and left me nearly dead.

You may notice that the rhymes are in the same places as before, and there's a single alliteration here: "kitten" and "kicked."

But, now that you know about assonance, you might also notice that I use it in each of these four lines; "lizard" and "flipped" both have a short "i" sound, as do "kitten" and "kicked," while "hamster" and "slammed" each have a short "a" sound, and "left" and "dead" each have a short "e" sound.

In case you would like to read the end of the poem, here it is:

> So, my advice? Avoid regrets;
> no matter what you do,
> don't ever let your family pets
> take lessons in kung fu.

When you write your own poems, I hope you'll take a moment as you rewrite and revise to think not just about the rhythm and rhymes, but also the other sound repetitions present in the words.

"Word Choices" by Margarita Engle

My word choices tend to be instinctive rather than planned. I love to write with a pen, listening as sounds flow onto paper. Many of my poems include assonance and internal rhymes rather than traditional end rhymes.

For my biographical picture book *Drum Dream Girl*, percussion was a key element. Alliteration and onomatopoeia played a natural role. Some parts of the long poem emphasize action: "Her hands seemed to fly / as they rippled / rapped / and pounded / all the rhythms / of her drum dreams." Other passages are about waiting for a chance to fulfill ambitions: "So the drum dream girl / had to keep dreaming / and drumming / alone." Above all, listening is the first skill the girl has to develop before she can become a skillful musician, so she walks in a park and hears "the whir of parrot wings / the clack of woodpecker beaks / the dancing tap / of her own footsteps / and the comforting pat / of her own heartbeat."

I can't say that any of these word choices were planned, but they were revised after my editor suggested that becoming a professional drummer could not have happened too easily, so I added "and she practiced / and she practiced / and she practiced."

The same can be said about me. Even after many years of publishing, I have to daydream, listen, take action, and practice, practice, practice before a poem can become a book.

"Example" by Nikki Grimes

When most authors use descriptive language in their writing, it often lengthens their text. But, as a poet, working in a more restricted format, I'm challenged to tell a story or paint a picture using as few words as possible. That makes my word selection more important than ever. I have less space to tell a story than other writers, so I must choose my words with precision because every word counts. Sometimes that requires adding words to a line for the sake of clarity, as I had to do in the golden shovel poem, "On Bully Patrol" from *One Last Word*.

My poems go through many revisions before I settle on my final word choice. Here's an example from an early draft of the poem.

> My girls limp home, feeble and frail
> from a week of hate-filled reproaches. "Come children."
> I pull each close, wipe away the tears of
> the day. Still, draped in sadness, sorrow
> clings to them like shadow. My sweet princesses dethroned.
> My heart-fingers feel the thorns of hate, pluck them one by
> one until my children smile again a
> rose rising in their warm, brown cheeks—a happy hue.

Here's a later revision. Note the word changes. I swap "girls" out for "youngest," and add "at school." The biggest change, though, is the descriptive "my heart-fingers." Here, I needed to lengthen the description to make it clearer, to paint a better picture. I changed it to "I shape my love like fingers," which worked much better.

> My youngest limp home, feeble and frail
> from a week of hate-filled reproaches at school. "Come, children."
> I pull each close, wipe away the tears of
> the day. Still, draped in sadness, sorrow
> clings to them like shadow. My sweet princesses dethroned.
> I shape my love like fingers, pluck out the thorns of hate, one by
> one, until my young ones smile again, a
> rose rising in their warm, brown cheeks—a happy hue.

The poem is almost there, but not quite. I still need to make it a little more personal and relatable to the reader. A change in pronoun will help that. I also got rid of "at school" because it was too obvious. I decided to go for something more meaningful, something with more of a punch. I changed "shadow" to "skin."

Why? Nothing clings more closely than one's own skin. I changed "thorns" to "splinters" because nothing is more continuously painful or annoying than a splinter lodged under the skin, and that's how racism feels. Lastly, "rose" became "glow" because dark complexions may glow, but they're not rosy in color. These final revisions did the trick.

> My youngest limps home, feeble and frail
> from a week of hate-filled reproaches aimed at dark children.
> I pull her close, wipe away the tears of
> the day. Still, draped in sadness, sorrow
> clings to her, like skin. My sweet princess, dethroned.
> I shape my love like fingers, pluck the splinters of hate, one by
> one, until my child smiles again, a
> glow rising in her warm, brown cheeks—a happy hue.

"Choice Words" by Obert Skye

For as long as my gray matter can remember, I have admired words. They often make it clear just what I'm thinking. That typed, however, I do harbor some resentment toward those words that do nothing but bore me.

I don't know the exact day or time my love of the literary first bloomed, or if I was dipped in a vat of alphabet-ink at birth. But I remember influences.

When I was a child, I was fortunate that, for the most part, I had fantastic teachers. Unfortunately, in third grade, I had an instructor who I just didn't connect with. He was kind, I'm sure, but he was dry to the point of old paint on a desert wall at high noon. I remember falling asleep once because everything he said was put so simply. We were told to "do our math," "read our pages," and "finish our lunch." His vocabulary never wavered and never impressed.

I had problems that year.

But, in fourth grade, I was blessed with a teacher who loved words. We were told to "soak up numbers and then let them drip out of us," "devour the pages of books like a meal and use the bookmark as a napkin," and "extract every bit of nutrient from each bit of our food our mouths accepted." She never asked us to pick up the room. Instead, she would say things like, "There is mischief about, be a hero and rescue this place from chaos."

I liked Ms. Jenkins.

My parents were similar. They seemed to have a desire to say things in a way that the last person I talked to hadn't. "How was school?" from my dad always came out as "Did you solve any mysteries today?" I broke my arm once falling off a chair and the bone split in three places. My mom didn't tell people I had a broken arm; she would say "my bones were just trying to be creative."

When I write now, I often find myself pausing for long bits to find the right words. Revision is my favorite part of the process, because I get to look at my first attempt, slash it up if needed, and plant something more fantastical in its place. I credit the books I have read as being the greatest contributor to my own vocabulary. And I blame the authors I admire as the reason I want to know more. It's a small delight when a word comes into my head that fits the mood of what I'm trying to convey. And it's a miracle when a perfect word choice conveys even more than I had hoped it would.

I am a person who would happily fight a whole day to procure the right word. The search and the reward are equally pleasing.

In conclusion: more words, please.

Author Biographies

Charles Ghigna ("Father Goose") lives in a treehouse in the middle of Alabama. He is the author of the award-winning *Strange Unusual Gross & Cool Animals* and more than one hundred other books from Time Inc., Random House, Simon & Schuster, Disney, Hyperion, Scholastic, Abrams, Boyds Mills Press, Charlesbridge, Capstone, Orca, and other publishers. He has written more than five thousand poems for children and adults that have appeared in anthologies, newspapers, and magazines, ranging from *The New Yorker* and *Harper's* to *Highlights* and *Cricket* magazines. He served as poet-in-residence and chair of creative writing at the Alabama School of Fine Arts, instructor of creative writing at Samford University, poetry editor of *English Journal* for the National Council of Teachers of English (NCTE) and as a nationally syndicated poetry feature writer for Tribune Media Services. He speaks at schools, conferences, libraries, and literary events throughout the US and overseas, and has read his poems at the Library of Congress, the John F. Kennedy Center for the Performing Arts, the American Library in Paris, the American School in Paris, and the International Schools of South America.

Jane Yolen is an author of almost 400 children's books. She ranges from picture books to fantasy and science fiction; from original fairy tales to historical novels. Her many books include *Owl Moon*, *The Devil's Arithmetic*, and *How Do Dinosaurs Say Goodnight?* She is also a poet, a teacher of writing and literature, and a reviewer of children's literature. She has been called the Hans Christian Andersen of America and the Aesop of the twentieth century. Jane Yolen's books and stories have won the Caldecott Medal, two Nebula Awards, two Christopher Medals, three World Fantasy Awards, three Mythopoeic Fantasy Awards, three Golden Kite Awards, the Jewish Book Award, the World Fantasy Association's Lifetime Achievement Award, and the Association of Jewish Libraries Award, among many others. Her website—http://janeyolen.com—presents information about her over three hundred books for children. It also contains essays, poems, answers to frequently asked questions, a brief biography, her travel schedule, and links to resources for teachers and writers. It is intended for children, teachers, writers, storytellers, and lovers of children's literature.

Janet Wong is a graduate of Yale Law School and a former lawyer who switched careers to become a children's author. Her dramatic career change has been featured on *The Oprah Winfrey Show*, CNN's *Paula Zahn Show*, and *Radical Sabbatical*. She is the author of more than 30 books for children and teens on a wide variety of subjects, including writing and revision (*You Have to Write*), diversity and community (*Apple Pie 4th of July*), peer pressure (*Me and Rolly Maloo*), chess (*Alex and the Wednesday Chess Club*), and yoga (*Twist: Yoga Poems*). A frequent featured speaker at literacy conferences, Wong has served as a member of several national committees, including the NCTE Poetry Committee and the ILA's Notable Books for a Global Society committee. Her current focus is encouraging children to publish their own writing using affordable new technologies.

The author of 200 titles for young readers, **Larry Dane Brimner** received the 2018 Robert F. Sibert Medal and the Carter G. Woodson Book Award for *Twelve Days in May: Freedom Ride 1961*. Best known for civil rights and social justice titles like *Black & White: The Confrontation between Reverend Fred L. Shuttlesworth and Eugene "Bull" Connor* (Carter G. Woodson Book Award; Robert F. Sibert Honor), *We Are One: The Story of Bayard Rustin* (Jane Addams Book Award), and *Birmingham Sunday* (Orbis Pictus Honor), he also writes picture book fiction. He taught at the high school and university levels in California for twenty years. His website is www.brimner.com.

Kenn Nesbitt—Former Children's Poet Laureate (2013–2015). Kenn Nesbitt has been writing humorous children's poetry for more than 25 years. He is the author of many books for kids, including *Kiss, Kiss Good Night*, *My Hippo Has the Hiccups*, and *Revenge of the Lunch Ladies*. His poems have appeared in numerous bestselling anthologies with more than two million copies in print. Kenn's work has been published in hundreds of magazines and school textbooks around the world, and his website, poetry4kids.com, is the most visited children's poetry website on the internet.

Margarita Engle is the Cuban American author of verse books such as *The Surrender Tree*, *Enchanted Air*, and *Drum Dream Girl*. Awards include the NSK Neustadt Prize, Astrid Lindgren Award Nomination, a Newbery Honor, multiple Pura Belpré, Walter, Américas, Jane Addams, and International Latino book awards and honors, as well as the Charlotte Zolotow, Golden Kite, Green Earth, Lee Bennett Hopkins, Arnold Adoff, and Claudia Lewis awards. Margarita served as the 2017–2019 Young People's Poet Laureate. Her most recent verse memoir is *Soaring Earth*. Her forthcoming books include *Dancing Hands*, *Dreams from Many Rivers*, and *With a Star in My Hand*. She was born in Los Angeles, but developed a deep attachment to her mother's homeland during childhood summers with relatives on the island. Margarita studied agronomy and botany along with creative writing. She lives in central California. Her website is www .margaritaengle.com.

New York Times bestselling author **Nikki Grimes** is the recipient of the 2017 Children's Literature Legacy Award, the 2016 Virginia Hamilton Literary Award, and the 2006 NCTE Award for Excellence in Poetry for Children. Her distinguished works include the much-honored books *Garvey's Choice*, ALA Notable book *What is Goodbye?*, Coretta Scott King Award winner *Bronx Masquerade*, and Coretta Scott King Author Honor books *Jazmin's Notebook*, *Talkin' About Bessie*, *Dark Sons*, *Words with Wings*, and *The Road to Paris*. Creator of the popular *Meet Danitra Brown*, Ms. Grimes lives in Corona, California.

Obert Skye is the best-selling and award-winning author of the Leven Thumps series, the Creature From My Closet series, the Pillage trilogy, Geeked Out, Wizard For Hire, and numerous other titles. He has sold millions of books to what must be millions of readers. Skye's books have been called "Hilarious," "Brilliant," and "Captivating." They've been called a few other things, but it would be rude to point those words out here.

Obert read his first book when he was two, wrote his first book when he was four, and was nearly trampled by a herd of water buffalo when he was six. He used to be allergic to cinnamon, and once played the lead in a play called Ships Ahoy.

Obert was born, he has grown up, and he is currently still living. He has called various points on the globe home—some of those points have been cool, some have been warm, but all have been pleasant.

Obert is married and has five children.

Appendix A

List of Lessons

Chapter	Page(s)	Word category	Lesson number and focus	Lesson duration	Appendix B resource (page, table, figure)
2	10–13	Acronyms	1. Defining acronyms	15 minutes	
	12–13		2. Acronym matching handout	20 minutes	99, Table B.1
	13		Independent practice (three activity options)	20 minutes	
	14–17	Antonyms	1. Nursery rhyme word substitution	30 minutes	100-101
	17		2. Word card matching	20 minutes	101, Table B.2
	17		Independent practice (three activity options)	30 minutes	101, Table B.2
	17–21	Eponyms	1. Eponym practice	20 minutes	102
	20		2. Eponym matching handout	15 minutes	103, Table B.3
	20–21		Independent practice (two activity options)	10–30 minutes	103
	21–26	Homonyms	1. Homophone poems	30 minutes	104, Table B.4
	24–25		2. Homograph poems, handout	20 minutes	105–6, Table B.5
	24–25		3. Homograph poem, word card matching	20 minutes	106
	26		Independent practice (two activity options)	30 minutes	107, Tables B.6 & B.7
	26–30	Retronym	1. Retronym story and poem, defining retronyms	30 minutes	108
	28–29		2. Inventions and retronyms	20 minutes	109, Table B.8
	29–30		Independent practice (two activity options)	30 minutes	109, Table B.8
	30–32	Synonym	1. Word lists, synonym paragraphs	20–30 minutes	110
	32		2. "We're Going On a Word Hunt" cards	15 minutes	111, Table B.9
	32–33		Independent practice	30 minutes	Figures 2.1 & 2.2
3	35–43	Similes	1. Defining similes	20 minutes	112, Table B.10
	39–40		2. A new comparison	30 minutes	113, Table B.11
	35–38		3. Explaining comparisons	30 minutes	
	38, 41–42		4. Over-the-top comparisons	20 minutes	114, Table B.12
	42		5. Over-the-top comparison paragraph	30 minutes	115
	43		Independent practice (option 1)	30 minutes	116, Table B.13
	43		Independent practice (option 2)	30 minutes	117, Table B.14

	43–49	Metaphors	1. Defining metaphors	20 minutes	118, Table B.15
	44		2. A new comparison	20 minutes	119, Table B.16
	43–44		3. Explaining comparisons	30 minutes	
	48		4. Over-the-top comparison	20 minutes	120, Table B.17
	48		5. Over-the-top comparison paragraph	30 minutes	121
	49		Independent practice (option 1)	30 minutes	122, Table B.18
	49		Independent practice (option 2)	30 minutes	122, Table B.19
4	51–67	Idioms	1. Defining idioms	20 minutes	124, Table B.20
	61		2. Idiom buddies' match	15 minutes	125, Table B.21
	61–62		3. In common idioms	20 minutes	126, Tables B.22 & B.23
	62–63		4. Idiom research	30 minutes	127
	64		5. Idiom illustration	20 minutes	128, Figure B.1
	64		6. "Out of the blue" and "flying colors" idiom story, "dog days of summer" idiom story	30 minutes	129–30
	64		7. Idiom story	20 minutes	131, Table B.24
	65		8. Story with made-up idioms, make your own idioms	20 minutes	132–33, Table B.25
	65		9. Story of a made-up idiom	30 minutes	134
	65		10. Idiom Readers Theater	40 minutes	135
	66		Independent practice (four activity options)	10–30 minutes	125
5	68–75	Shades of meaning	1. David's witch narrative; handout	30 minutes	136–38
	74–75		2. Practice with Aesop's fables for shades of meaning	30 minutes	139
	75		3. Shades of meaning buddy match; handout	30 minutes	140–41, Table B.26
	75		4. Sorting shades of meaning	20 minutes	142, Table B.27
	76		Independent practice (two activity options)	20–30 minutes	143
	76–81	Word origins	1. "I've Got a Secret"	20 minutes	144–45, Tables B.28 & B.29
	80		2. Word origin partner match	20 minutes	146–47, Tables B.30–B.32
	80–81		3. Word trees	40 minutes	148–49, Figures B.2 & B.3
	81		Independent practice (three activity options)	20–30 minutes	150

Appendix B

Lesson Resources

Acronym Lesson 2

Name: _____

Can you figure out which name or phrase matches each acronym? Draw a line connecting each acronym and the correct name or phrase.

TABLE B.1. Acronym Matching Game

Acronym	Name/Phrase
EPCOT	President of the United States
LASER	self-contained underwater breathing apparatus
LEGO	random access memory
NABISCO	zone improvement plan
POTUS	sound navigation and ranging
RAM	light amplification by stimulated emission of radiation
SCUBA	Experimental Prototype Community of Tomorrow
SONAR	*leg godt*, Danish for "play well"
ZIP (code)	National Biscuit Company

Empowering Students' Knowledge of Vocabulary: Learning How Language Works, Grades 3–5 by Mary Jo Fresch and David L. Harrison © 2020 NCTE.

Antonym Lesson 1

Nursery Rhymes That Might Have Been
By David L. Harrison

An antonym's the opposite
Of what we mean to say.
Sometimes it makes it *better*!
But it might be *worse* that way.

Mary's lamb was not so *small*,
As Mother Goose would inform us.
The antonym would have us know
The lamb was quite *enormous*.

A Nursery Rhyme Changed by Antonyms

Mary Had a Little Lamb

Mary had an enormous lamb
Its fleece was black as tar,
And everywhere that Mary came,
The lamb was never thar.

Other Nursery Rhymes Changed by Antonyms

Jack and Jill

Jack and Jill strolled down the hill
To take a pail of dirt.
Jack jumped up and fixed his crown
And Jill went tumbling first.

Old King Cole

Young Queen Cole
Was a sour young soul
And a sour young soul was she.
She whispered for her pipe
And she whispered for her bowl
And she whispered for her drummers three.

Empowering Students' Knowledge of Vocabulary: Learning How Language Works, Grades 3–5 by Mary Jo Fresch and David L. Harrison © 2020 NCTE.

Antonym Lesson 2

Materials

- word cards—print, cut apart, and distribute to students

TABLE B.2. Antonym Word Cards

big	small	over	under
right	left	old	new
tall	short	fast	slow
give	take	stop	go
sad	happy	hot	cold
wet	dry	sit	stand
always	never	shrink	swell

Empowering Students' Knowledge of Vocabulary: Learning How Language Works, Grades 3–5 by Mary Jo Fresch and David L. Harrison © 2020 NCTE.

Eponym Lesson 1

I saw a guy with long sideburns wearing a cardigan riding on a Ferris wheel eating a jumbo sandwich and a Baby Ruth.

I saw a *guy*
with long *sideburns*
wearing a *cardigan*
riding on a *Ferris wheel*
eating a *jumbo*
sandwich
and a *Baby Ruth*.

Empowering Students' Knowledge of Vocabulary: Learning How Language Works, Grades 3–5 by Mary Jo Fresch and David L. Harrison © 2020 NCTE.

Eponym Lesson 2

Name: _____

Can you figure out which name matches to each eponym? Draw a line connecting the eponym and the correct name.

TABLE B.3. Eponym Matching Game

Eponym	Name
frisbee	Reverend Sylvester Graham
Ferris wheel	General Ambrose Burnside
silhouette	Jules Léotard
sandwich	Frisbie Pie Company
dunce	Friedrich Ludwig Dobermann
leotard	Harold "Matt" Matson and Elliot Handler
sideburns	John Duns Scotus
Mattel	Étienne de Silhouette
Doberman Pinscher	George Washington Gale Ferris Jr.
graham cracker	Earl of Sandwich

Empowering Students' Knowledge of Vocabulary: Learning How Language Works, Grades 3–5 by Mary Jo Fresch and David L. Harrison © 2020 NCTE.

Homonym Lesson 1

Homophone
By David L. Harrison

Need a word to make a rhyme?
Be careful what you choose.
A homophone is simply knot
The nym you want to use.

TABLE B.4. "The Party" Chart

"The Party"	Correct spelling	The corrected poem
I dawned clean genes		I donned clean jeans
and died my hare.		and dyed my hair.
I gnu that I wood		I knew that I would
sea ewe their		see you there
I looked but yew		I looked but you
Weren't they're my deer,		Weren't there my dear,
And sew I left		And so I left
Two come back hear.		To come back here.

Empowering Students' Knowledge of Vocabulary: Learning How Language Works, Grades 3–5 by Mary Jo Fresch and David L. Harrison © 2020 NCTE.

Homograph
By David L. Harrison

Duck can mean to "duck!"
Or go "quack-quack."
A joke can be a mess
Or make us laugh.
Back can mean "your back"
Or "going back."
And that's what makes
A homograph a homograph.

In a Jam
By David L. Harrison

He spilled the jam
all down his pants,
and now he pants,
"I'm in a jam!"

He scraped with sticks
and fingernails
as hard as nails,
but jam sticks.

His dog licked
away the jam
and solved his jam
so he's not licked.

Empowering Students' Knowledge of Vocabulary: Learning How Language Works, Grades 3–5 by Mary Jo Fresch and David L. Harrison © 2020 NCTE.

Name: _____

Read the sentence in the first column. In the third column, write the definition of the word in the middle column.

TABLE B.5. "In a Jam" Chart

Sentence	Homograph	Definition
He spilled the jam	jam	
"I'm in a jam!"	jam	
all down his pants	pants	
and now he pants,	pants	
He scraped with sticks	sticks	
but jam sticks	sticks	
His dog licked	licked	
so he's not licked.	licked	

Empowering Students' Knowledge of Vocabulary: Learning How Language Works, Grades 3–5 by Mary Jo Fresch and David L. Harrison © 2020 NCTE.

Homonym Lesson 3

A Peculiar Event
By David L. Harrison

I was tying my shoelace in a bow,
preparing to row from the bow,
when a dove dove down
and frightened the geese
and caused an enormous row.

A bullfrog sang, as a bullfrog does,
in a bass voice deeper than a cow.
A bass made a splash
that startled two does.
All in all quite a row in the bow.

Materials

- word cards—print and cut apart to distribute to students

TABLE B.6. Homonym Word Cards

read	lead	tear	wind
moped	does	live	sewer
bow	dove	use	close
produce	bass	wound	minute

TABLE B.7. Homonym Riddle: Word Pairs

be, bee	blue, blew	write/right	rode/road	tail/tale
mail/male	some/sum	hair/hare	knot/not	where/wear
dough/doe	Jim/gym	flea/flee	mane/main/Maine	sweet/suite
bye/buy	sea/see	sale/sail	fur/fir	peace/piece

Empowering Students' Knowledge of Vocabulary: Learning How Language Works, Grades 3–5 by Mary Jo Fresch and David L. Harrison © 2020 NCTE.

Retronym Lesson 1

A book used to be just a book. Water was water. A phone was a phone. Mail was mail. But times change. A retronym is a word that used to stand alone but now we need to give it some help to make sure everyone knows what we're talking about.

These days, we might call a book a book in print or a hardback or paperback because otherwise someone might think we're talking about an audio book, a digital book, or an e-book. Water? If we don't say "regular" water or maybe "tap" water, people might think we're talking about bottled water. A phone is a smart phone or a cell phone. A plain old phone phone? Now we call it a land line. Mail that comes with stamps and lands in our mailbox? "Snail" mail. Otherwise, what do we have? The kind of mail we get on our computers!

So water isn't water
if it isn't from a tap,
and a plain old book
must have a retronym.
Unless a line is landed then
it's probably a cell.
And mail without a nym?
Odds are slim.

Defining Retronyms

Names: _____

Why are these words retronyms? What change in our life, history, or invention made it necessary to create the following retronyms?

1. analog watch
2. bar soap
3. brick-and-mortar stores
4. corn on the cob
5. cloth diaper
6. hardwired
7. live music
8. push lawnmower
9. silent movie
10. whole milk

Empowering Students' Knowledge of Vocabulary: Learning How Language Works, Grades 3–5 by Mary Jo Fresch and David L. Harrison © 2020 NCTE.

Retronym Lesson 2

Name: _____

Fill in the table—explain about the invention and what retronym we might need to add to our language.

TABLE B.8. Invention–Retronym

Invention	What is it?	What retronym might need to be used due to this invention?
Driverless car		
Front load washer		
Flat screen television		
Smart watch		
Electric toothbrush		

Empowering Students' Knowledge of Vocabulary: Learning How Language Works, Grades 3–5 by Mary Jo Fresch and David L. Harrison © 2020 NCTE.

Synonym Lesson 1
Word Lists
- *walk*—stroll, saunter, amble, trudge, plod, dawdle, hike, tramp, tromp, slog, stomp, trek, march, stride, sashay, glide, troop, patrol, wander, ramble, tread, prowl, promenade, roam, traipse, stretch one's legs, mosey, hoof it, perambulate
- *sky*—azure, celestial sphere, empyrean, firmament, heavens, the blue, upper atmosphere, vault, wild blue yonder
- *blue*—sky blue, azure, cobalt, sapphire, navy, powder blue, midnight blue, Prussian blue, electric blue, indigo, royal blue, ice-blue, baby blue, air force blue, robin's egg blue, peacock blue, ultramarine, aquamarine, steel blue, slate blue, cyan, Oxford blue, Cambridge blue, cerulean
- *whistle*—blare, blast, fife, flute, pipe, shriek, signal, sound, toot, tootle, trill, warble

Paragraphs

1. One day, I went *walking*. The *sky* was *blue*. I *whistled* a happy tune as I *walked* along.

2. One day, I went *perambulating*. The *firmament* was *cerulean*. I *shrieked* a happy tune as I *promenaded* along.

3. One day, I went *sashaying*. The *wild blue yonder* was *cyan*. I *blasted* a happy tune as I *wandered* along.

4. One day, I went *patrolling*. The *upper atmosphere* was *celestial*. I *tootled* a happy tune as I *dawdled* along.

Empowering Students' Knowledge of Vocabulary: Learning How Language Works, Grades 3–5 by Mary Jo Fresch and David L. Harrison © 2020 NCTE.

Synonym Lesson 2

Materials

- "We're Going on a Word Hunt" cards—copy and cut apart

TABLE B.9. "We're Going on a Word Hunt" Cards

I have the first card. We're going on a word hunt for a synonym for *big*.	I found *large*. We're going on a word hunt for a synonym for *car*.
I found *automobile*. We're going on a word hunt for a synonym for *begin*.	I found *start*. We're going on a word hunt for a synonym for *round*.
I found *circular*. We're going on a word hunt for a synonym for *small*.	I found *tiny*. We're going on a word hunt for a synonym for *gift*.
I found *present*. We're going on a word hunt for a synonym for *center*.	I found *middle*. We're going on a word hunt for a synonym for *laugh*.
I found *giggle*. We're going on a word hunt for a synonym for *rabbit*.	I found *bunny*. We're going on a word hunt for a synonym for *rug*.
I found *carpet*. We're going on a word hunt for a synonym for *end*.	I found *finish* and I am the last card!

Empowering Students' Knowledge of Vocabulary: Learning How Language Works, Grades 3–5 by Mary Jo Fresch and David L. Harrison © 2020 NCTE.

Simile Lesson 1

Defining Similes

TABLE B.10. List of Similes

As cold as ice
As blind as a bat
As hard as a rock
As white as a ghost
As smooth as silk
As sweet as sugar
As clean as a whistle
As strong as an ox
As nutty as a fruitcake
As cool as a cucumber

Definition of a simile:

Empowering Students' Knowledge of Vocabulary: Learning How Language Works, Grades 3–5 by Mary Jo Fresch and David L. Harrison © 2020 NCTE.

Simile Lesson 2

A New Comparison

TABLE B.11. Similes with New Comparisons

The first thing	The usual worn-out comparison	A new comparison	Because
As cold as _____	ice	snow	
As blind as a _____	bat	stick	
As hard as a _____	rock	fist	
As white as a _____	ghost	chalk	
As smooth as _____	silk		
As sweet as _____	sugar		
As clean as a _____	whistle		
As strong as an _____	ox		
As nutty as a _____	fruitcake		
As cool as a _____	cucumber		

Empowering Students' Knowledge of Vocabulary: Learning How Language Works, Grades 3–5 by Mary Jo Fresch and David L. Harrison © 2020 NCTE.

Simile Lesson 4

Over-the-Top Comparisons

TABLE B.12. Over-the-Top Comparison Similes

The first thing	The usual worn-out comparison	An over-the-top comparison
As cold as _____	ice	a six-pack of frozen mackerel after two years in the freezer
As blind as a _____	bat	a rhinoceros horn covered with a sack of bad potatoes
As hard as _____	a rock	prying out a concrete filling with a toothpick
As white as _____	ghost	four-ply toilet paper made from aspen trees
As smooth as _____	silk	
As sweet as _____	sugar	
As clean as a _____	whistle	
As strong as an _____	ox	
As nutty as a _____	fruitcake	
As cool as a _____	cucumber	

Empowering Students' Knowledge of Vocabulary: Learning How Language Works, Grades 3–5 by Mary Jo Fresch and David L. Harrison © 2020 NCTE.

Simile Lesson 5

Paragraph of "Over-the-Top" Comparisons

One winter day, I got caught walking in a blizzard. It was as cold as a six-pack of frozen mackerel after two years in the freezer and the swirling snow was as white as four-ply toilet paper made from aspen trees. All that snow made me as blind as a rhinoceros horn covered with a sack of bad potatoes. Walking into the wind was as hard as prying out a concrete filling with a toothpick. I thought I'd never get home.

Empowering Students' Knowledge of Vocabulary: Learning How Language Works, Grades 3–5 by Mary Jo Fresch and David L. Harrison © 2020 NCTE.

Similes: Independent Practice

Name: _____

Complete this chart just as we did the one in class together. Be sure to write full sentences in the "Because" column.

TABLE B.13. Worn-Out Similes with New Comparisons and Over-the-Top Comparisons: Because

The first thing	The usual worn-out comparison	A new comparison	Because	Over-the-top comparison
As brave as	a lion			
As busy as	a bee			
As cunning as	a fox			
As dry as	a bone			
As good as	gold			
As light as	a feather			
As slow as	a tortoise			
As strong as	an ox			

Empowering Students' Knowledge of Vocabulary: Learning How Language Works, Grades 3–5 by Mary Jo Fresch and David L. Harrison © 2020 NCTE.

Similes: Independent Practice

Name: _____

Choose a simile and write it in the first box. Rewrite the simile with a new comparison or an over-the-top comparison.

TABLE B.14. Similes with New Comparisons or Over-the-Top Comparisons

Simile	A new comparison or an "over-the-top" comparison

Illustrate your new simile:

Empowering Students' Knowledge of Vocabulary: Learning How Language Works, Grades 3–5 by Mary Jo Fresch and David L. Harrison © 2020 NCTE.

Metaphor Lesson 1

Defining Metaphors

TABLE B.15. Example Metaphors

You're a chicken.
Mom says my room is a compost heap.
Daddy calls me his angel.
Today, the clouds are balls of cotton.
You are my sunshine.
Life is a roller coaster.
Her brain is a computer.
My big brother is a couch potato.
He is a walking dictionary.

Define metaphor:

Empowering Students' Knowledge of Vocabulary: Learning How Language Works, Grades 3–5 by Mary Jo Fresch and David L. Harrison © 2020 NCTE.

Metaphor Lesson 2

A New Comparison

TABLE B.16. Metaphors with New Comparisons

The first thing	The usual worn-out comparison	A new comparison	Because
You're a	chicken	cowardly lion	
Mom says my room is a	disaster	compost heap	
Daddy calls me his	angel	sweet thang	
Today, the clouds are	balls of cotton	cream puffs	
You are my	sunshine		
Life is a	roller coaster		
Her brain is a	computer		
My big brother is a	couch potato		
He is a walking	dictionary		

Empowering Students' Knowledge of Vocabulary: Learning How Language Works, Grades 3–5 by Mary Jo Fresch and David L. Harrison © 2020 NCTE.

Metaphor Lesson 4

Over-the-Top Comparisons

TABLE B.17. Over-the-Top Comparison Metaphors

The first thing	The usual worn-out comparison	An over-the-top comparison
You're a	chicken	spineless piece of string about five feet long
Mom says my room is	disaster	the movie set from *The Night the Dragon Fought T. Rex*
Daddy calls me his	angel	divinityfudgepuddingchocolatemintsweetypie
Today, the clouds are	balls of cotton	what you get when you shoot marshmallows out of a cannon
You are my	sunshine	thingamajig that makes my heart go boing
Life is a	roller coaster	
Her brain is a	computer	
My big brother is a	couch potato	
He is a walking	dictionary	

Empowering Students' Knowledge of Vocabulary: Learning How Language Works, Grades 3–5 by Mary Jo Fresch and David L. Harrison © 2020 NCTE.

Metaphor Lesson 5

It's one of those days when the clouds are what you get when you shoot marsh-mallows out of a cannon and I'm thinking about my family. My brother calls me a spineless piece of string about five feet long and Mom says my room is the movie set from *The Night the Dragon Fought T. Rex*, but Daddy calls me his divini-tyfudgepuddingchocolatemintsweetypie and my sister goes through the house singing, "You're my thingamajig that makes my heart go boing." I think my family is strange. I'm going out to play.

Empowering Students' Knowledge of Vocabulary: Learning How Language Works, Grades 3–5 by Mary Jo Fresch and David L. Harrison © 2020 NCTE.

Metaphors: Independent Practice

Name: _____

Complete this chart just as we did the one in class together! Be sure to write full sentences in the "Because" column.

TABLE B.18. Worn-Out Metaphors with New Comparisons and Over-the-Top Comparisons: Because

The first thing	The usual worn-out comparison	A new comparison	Because	Over-the-top comparison
The cafeteria was	a zoo today.			
My teacher	is an angel.			
The library computer	is a dinosaur.			
He is a	night owl.			
The ballerina was	a swan gliding across the stage.			
My uncle is	a road hog.			
The lawn is	a green carpet.			
Her long hair was	a flowing river.			
The lake was	a mirror.			
The friends were	two peas in a pod.			

Empowering Students' Knowledge of Vocabulary: Learning How Language Works, Grades 3–5 by Mary Jo Fresch and David L. Harrison © 2020 NCTE.

Metaphors: Independent Practice

Name: _____

Choose a metaphor and write it in the first box. Rewrite the metaphor with a new comparison or an "over-the-top" comparison.

TABLE B.19. Metaphors with New Comparisons or Over-the-Top Comparisons

Metaphor	A new comparison or an "over-the-top" comparison

Illustrate your new metaphor:

Empowering Students' Knowledge of Vocabulary: Learning How Language Works, Grades 3–5 by Mary Jo Fresch and David L. Harrison © 2020 NCTE.

Idiom Lesson 1

TABLE B.20. Defining and Using Idioms

Idiom	Meaning of idiom	Sentence
Apple of my eye		
Bury the hatchet		
In the nick of time		
Nest egg		
Sleep tight		

Define idiom:

Empowering Students' Knowledge of Vocabulary: Learning How Language Works, Grades 3–5 by Mary Jo Fresch and David L. Harrison © 2020 NCTE.

Idiom Lesson 2

Materials

- game cards—photocopy and cut apart to distribute

TABLE B.21. Idioms, Meanings, and Origins

Idiom	Meaning	Origin
Apple of my eye	favorite or pet	As far back as the ninth century, the pupil of the eye was considered an important spot of our anatomy. The pupil was apple shaped, and because it was so vital to life, anything precious (such as loved ones) was called the apple of their eye.
Blind as a bat	unable to see problems	For many centuries, people thought bats were blind due to their flight patterns. However, we now know they use echolocation to find their way, but the idiom has stuck with us.
Bury the hatchet	settle their differences	Native Americans would not declare peace between warring tribes until all the warriors had literally buried their hatchets. If this peace was not lasting, the tomahawks were unearthed.
Couch potato	to be idle	This idiom started in the 1970s. This describes a person who vegetates in front of the television. When someone sits, watches, and eats, they supposedly begin to look like a potato.
Go whole hog	go the whole way	In the eighteenth and nineteenth centuries, an Irish shilling was called a "hog." This was equal to an American ten-cent piece. A person willing to spend the entire shilling went whole hog.
In the nick of time	just in time	Prior to pocket watches and timepieces, time at sporting events were kept track using a "nick-stick." The nick-stick was used as a way to tally a period of time.
Limelight	center of attention	In the early 1800s, Thomas Drummond discovered that when calcium oxide (lime) is heated it gives off a glaring white light. So, this limelight was used in lighthouses and later in theaters.
Nest egg	saving for the future	Farmers found that hens were more likely to lay eggs if other eggs were already in the nest. Clever farmers placed a small porcelain egg in the nest. The result was extra eggs that provided a profit. The extra money was set aside and called a "nest egg."
Sleep tight	sleep well	In Colonial times, mattresses were held up to bed frames through a crisscrossing of ropes. These needed to be tightened occasionally, or the mattress would sag.
Under the weather	sick	On ships, sailors would go below to their cabins to try to avoid getting sick when the weather started getting rough. These seamen quite literally were going under, or away from, the weather.

Empowering Students' Knowledge of Vocabulary: Learning How Language Works, Grades 3–5 by Mary Jo Fresch and David L. Harrison © 2020 NCTE.

Idiom Lesson 3

Materials

- idiom cards—cut and distribute the 12 boxes below to each small group

TABLE B.22. Idiom Grouping Game

Sitting duck	Cat nap	Charley horse
Get back on the horse	Like a duck to water	Raining cats and dogs
When the cat's away	Don't look a gift horse in the mouth	Cat got your tongue
Ducks in a row	Lucky duck	Work like a horse

Answers

Read aloud or provide copies for students to self-check.

TABLE B.23. Idiom Grouping Game: Answers

Sitting duck	**Cat nap**	**Charley horse**
someone or something with no protection against danger	A short sleep	A muscle cramp, most often in the legs
Get back on the horse	**Like a duck to water**	**Raining cats and dogs**
To try again	a natural talent	Very heavy rain
When the cat's away	**Don't look a gift horse in the mouth**	**Cat got your tongue**
When no one is in charge some people will do whatever they want	Show lack of appreciation for a gift or something else received for no cost	Someone not speaking very much or at all
Ducks in a row	**Lucky duck**	**Work like a horse**
well organized	someone with good luck	Work very hard, with great energy and persistence

Empowering Students' Knowledge of Vocabulary: Learning How Language Works, Grades 3–5 by Mary Jo Fresch and David L. Harrison © 2020 NCTE.

Idiom Lesson 4

Investigating Idioms: Answers

Name: _____

Idiom:

Meaning:

Example of idiom in a sentence:

Story of the origin of this idiom:

Empowering Students' Knowledge of Vocabulary: Learning How Language Works, Grades 3–5 by Mary Jo Fresch and David L. Harrison © 2020 NCTE.

Idiom Lesson 5

Investigating Idioms: Illustration

Idiom: dog days of summer

Meaning: hottest days of the summer

Example of idiom in a sentence: "We love going to the pool when we are sweating through the dog days of summer."

Story of the origin of this idiom: Sirius, a star in the Canis Major constellation, appears in early morning in the summer. In ancient Roman times, people thought that star sent extra heat to earth, thus making us hotter. We were in the "dog days."

Illustrate the idiom:

FIGURE B.1. *Dog Days of Summer* by MJF.

Empowering Students' Knowledge of Vocabulary: Learning How Language Works, Grades 3–5 by Mary Jo Fresch and David L. Harrison © 2020 NCTE.

Idiom Lesson 6

A Story about "Out of the Blue" and "Flying Colors" by David L. Harrison

A challenge that is both entertaining and instructive is to search for the origins of idioms. For example, what did "out of the blue" originally mean? This one isn't too hard. Let's say we have a beautiful day with a blue sky. Suddenly a fierce thunderstorm strikes—totally unexpected—out of the blue. So when we say a thing happened "out of the blue," we mean much the same thing. The thing that happened was totally unexpected.

How about "with flying colors?" Colors used to be another name for the flags on ships meant to identify the ship or country of origin. When a ship sailed into port with its flags (colors) flying, it had returned successfully from its mission. If you pass a test with flying colors, congratulations. You have returned triumphantly from a great journey at sea! Of course what we mean these days is that you were successful at something. You were triumphant. You passed the test!

Another benefit of searching for the origins of idioms is that you never know what interesting story-starters you'll find. When I read about a ship's colors, I can imagine a story about a lonely boy waiting for his father to return from the sea and who spends much of each day on a hill where he will be more likely to spot the flag on his father's ship. How long has the father been gone? How old is the boy? Why is he alone? Is his father okay? Is he really going to make it home? Will the boy go with his father on his next voyage? Will the boy somehow rescue his father? Will his father bring him a present? Just like that a simple search for the origin of "with flying colors" slips into a bank of ideas to write about.

Empowering Students' Knowledge of Vocabulary: Learning How Language Works, Grades 3–5 by Mary Jo Fresch and David L. Harrison © 2020 NCTE.

A Story about "Dog Days of Summer" by Mary Jo Fresch

My poor dog, Spotty, was lying in the shade, panting away. It was so hot outside we could not walk barefoot on our driveway. My Nana came out of the house with a bowl of water.

"Be sure Spotty drinks some water," she said. "These dog days of summer are sure hot!"

"Nana, what do you mean? These are Spotty's days?" I asked.

"No, 'dog days' means it's a really hot part of the summer. Back in Roman times, people saw the Sirius star in the morning in the summertime. They thought that star made them extra hot. As the star was from the Canis Major, they called it 'dog days.'"

"Dog? For a star?" I asked.

"Yes," replied Nana. "You know how we say dogs are canines? That constellation's name means 'great dog,' because, in Greek mythology, he was one of Orion's hunting dogs."

"Wow," I exclaimed. "Better give me that water bowl—and I'll take a lemonade, please!"

"Coming right up," sang Nana.

Idiom Lesson 7

TABLE B.24. Idioms–Story Chart

Idiom list	David's story
Out of the blue Hadn't cracked a book	"<u>Out of the blue</u>, teacher gave us a math test," my friend groaned. "And I hadn't even <u>cracked a book</u> to study."
Felt like your goose was cooked	"Oh no!" I said. "<u>Your goose was cooked!</u>"
In hot water Like a bird brain See eye to eye	"I <u>was in hot water</u> for sure," he agreed. "Sometimes, I think teacher thinks <u>I'm a bird brain</u>. We <u>don't always see eye to eye</u>."
Fingers crossed	"You must have <u>had your fingers crossed</u>?" I said.
Had mixed feelings	"Let's just say <u>I had mixed feelings</u>," he sighed.
In the same boat	"But wasn't the whole class <u>in the same boat</u>?" I asked.
A gray area Smart as a whip	"Well that's <u>a gray area</u>," my friend said. "Some of the other kids in there are <u>as smart as a whip</u>."
I'm all ears	"What happened?" I asked. "I'm <u>all ears</u>."
With flying colors I aced it	"I passed the test <u>with flying colors!</u>" he laughed. "I <u>aced it!</u>"
Gotten your act together	"Wow!" I said. "You must have really <u>gotten your act together</u>."
He drew a blank As cool as a cucumber Gave it a shot Nailed it As easy as ABC In the bag	"For a while, I <u>drew a blank</u> on the first problem," he admitted. "But I stayed <u>cool as a cucumber</u>. I <u>gave it a shot</u> and <u>nailed it</u>. The rest was <u>as easy as ABC</u>. I knew then I had it <u>in the bag</u>."
A piece of cake	"A <u>piece of cake</u>," I laughed.
Icing on the cake	"And getting an A was <u>the icing on the cake</u>," he laughed back.

Empowering Students' Knowledge of Vocabulary: Learning How Language Works, Grades 3–5 by Mary Jo Fresch and David L. Harrison © 2020 NCTE.

Idiom Lesson 8

TABLE B.25. Stories: Original Idioms–Made-Up Idioms

David's first story	David's story of made-up idioms
"<u>Out of the blue</u>, teacher gave us a math test," my friend groaned. "And I hadn't even <u>cracked a book</u> to study."	"<u>Like a runaway cat</u>, teacher gave us a math test," my friend groaned. "And I hadn't even <u>boiled eggs</u> to study."
"Oh no!" I said. "<u>Your goose was cooked!</u>"	"Oh no!" I said. "<u>Your belt must have broken!</u>"
"I <u>was in hot water</u> for sure," he agreed. "Sometimes, I think teacher thinks <u>I'm a bird brain</u>. We <u>don't always see eye to eye</u>."	"I <u>couldn't see the clouds</u>," he agreed. "Sometimes, I think teacher thinks <u>I'm a T. Rex tail</u>. We <u>don't always sing in the same room</u>."
"You must have <u>had your fingers crossed</u>?" I said.	"You must have <u>blown your balloon</u>?" I said.
"Let's just say <u>I had mixed feelings</u>," he sighed.	"Let's just say <u>I emptied the bucket</u>," he sighed.
"But wasn't the whole class <u>in the same boat</u>?" I asked.	"But wasn't the whole class <u>shaggier than a goat</u>?" I asked.
"Well that's <u>a gray area</u>," my friend said. "Some of the other kids in there are <u>as smart as a whip</u>."	"Well that's <u>for a whale to blow</u>," my friend said. "Some of the other kids in there are <u>as gritty as cereal</u>."
"What happened?" I asked. "I'm <u>all ears</u>."	"What happened?" I asked. "I'm <u>falling down</u>."
"I passed the test <u>with flying colors</u>!" he laughed. "I <u>aced it</u>!"	"I passed the test <u>over two mountains</u>!" he laughed. "I <u>wore the cap</u>!"
"Wow!" I said. "You must have really <u>gotten your act together</u>."	"Wow!" I said. "You must have really gotten <u>settled sideways</u>."
"For a while, I <u>drew a blank</u> on the first problem," he admitted. "But I stayed <u>cool as a cucumber</u>. I <u>gave it a shot</u> and <u>nailed it</u>. The rest was <u>as easy as ABC</u>. I knew then I had it <u>in the bag</u>."	"For a while, I <u>considered rocks</u> on the first problem," he admitted. "But I stayed <u>bad as water</u>. I <u>threw it high</u> and <u>peeled the whole orange</u>. The rest was <u>history in the future</u>. I knew then I had it <u>served over rice</u>."
"A <u>piece of cake</u>," I laughed.	"A <u>spike in the hand</u>," I laughed.
"And getting an A was <u>the icing on the cake</u>," he laughed back.	"And getting an A was <u>outwrestling snakes</u>," he laughed back.

Empowering Students' Knowledge of Vocabulary: Learning How Language Works, Grades 3–5 by Mary Jo Fresch and David L. Harrison © 2020 NCTE.

Make Your Own Idioms

Name: _____

Replace the crossed-out word with a new word. What new idiom can you create? The first one is done for you.

The ~~dog~~ ice cream days of summer.
Apple of my ~~eye~~ _____.
Bury the ~~hatchet~~ _____.
In the ~~nick~~_____ of time.
~~Nest~~ _____ egg.
Sleep ~~tight~~ _____.
When the ~~cat's~~ _____ away.
Cat's got your ~~tongue~~ _____.
Lucky ~~duck~~ _____.
Get back on the ~~horse~~ _____.
Raining ~~cats and dogs~~ _____.

Idiom Lesson 9

Origin of "Like a Runaway Cat" by David L. Harrison

In 1294, an Irish pub keeper owned a cat that everyone agreed was the orneriest cat anyone had ever seen. That cat's favorite trick was to sneak up on a customer, scratch his ankle, and dash away, leaving the poor victim as surprised as a runaway cat. Today "like a runaway cat" is used to mean, well, out of the blue.

Origin of "Ice Cream Days of Summer" by Mary Jo Fresch

One August day in 55 CE, the Roman ruler Nero Claudius Caesar, sighed so loudly his servants came running. He told them he was so hot that he couldn't stand another day of summer! His servants got together, hoping to think of a way to make their emperor happy. One servant, Benjerry, suggested they run up into the mountains and get snow. They could add the juice of figs to make the snow a cold, tasty treat. The plan worked! Caesar was so happy that he declared every August (the month named for the first Roman Emperor) shall be called the "ice cream days of summer."

Empowering Students' Knowledge of Vocabulary: Learning How Language Works, Grades 3–5 by Mary Jo Fresch and David L. Harrison © 2020 NCTE.

Idiom Lesson 10

Readers Theater Script

NARRATOR: Welcome to August 55 CE.

NERO CLAUDIUS CAESAR: (*sighs loudly*)

(*Servants come running in.*)

NERO CLAUDIUS CAESAR: I am so hot, I can't stand another day of summer.

(*Servants get together, whispering.*)

BENJERRY: I know—we'll run up into the mountains and get snow! We can add the juice of figs to make a cold, tasty treat.

(*One of the servants hands Nero Claudius Caesar a bowl.*)

NERO CLAUDIUS CAESAR: Benjerry, I'm so happy! I hereby declare that every August, the month named for our first Roman Emperor, shall be called the "ice cream days of summer."

(*Everyone cheers.*)

Empowering Students' Knowledge of Vocabulary: Learning How Language Works, Grades 3–5 by Mary Jo Fresch and David L. Harrison © 2020 NCTE.

Shades of Meaning Lesson 1

Original "Witch" Narrative

A witch was flying through a terrible storm. It was nighttime. She wasn't afraid. She was laughing.

David's Revised "Witch" Narrative

Huge storm clouds filled the sky. When lightning flashed, you could see a witch flying among the clouds. You could hear her laughing above the sound of thunder. Far below, everything was quiet. But, up high, the storm was howling. It was a good night for Sally the witch to go flying. She felt reckless. She yelled happily as she flew.

David's Second Revision of the "Witch" Narrative

Clouds were volcanoes erupting in the night. A blue-white tongue of lightning crackled across the sky. Cackling merrily, a darting form swooped and glided like a bony, black bird. A double loop. A slow roll. A graceful dive. Shrill laughter rang out above rumbling thunder. Thirty thousand feet below, the world was sleeping. Up here, a delicious brew was boiling. A perfect night for a witch to play tag with lightning and slide down cloud mountains. Xxxxlntz, or "Sally" as she was sometimes called, loved every thump and crash of it. Throwing caution to the wind, she shrieked with joy, happier than a toad in a mud puddle. (Adapted from Graham, 1976, p. 48.)

Using what we've been learning about, David:

- replaced "Huge storm clouds" with a *metaphor*: "Clouds were volcanoes"
- replaced "filled" with a stronger *synonym*: "erupting"
- replaced "flashed" with a stronger *synonym*: "crackled"
- gave lightning a *metaphor*: "blue-white tongue"
- replaced "witch flying" with more action words and a *simile*: "darting form swooped and glided like a bony black bird"
- replaced "laughing" with stronger *synonym*: "cackling"
- provided details of how Sally is having fun: "Double loop. Slow roll. Graceful dive"
- replaced "storm" with a surprising *metaphor*: "delicious brew"

Empowering Students' Knowledge of Vocabulary: Learning How Language Works, Grades 3–5 by Mary Jo Fresch and David L. Harrison © 2020 NCTE.

- replaced "howling" with a more related *synonym*: "brewing"

- used a *metaphor* for clouds: "mountains"

- gave Sally a more appropriate witch name: "Xxxxlntz"

- showed how "reckless" Sally was with an *idiom*: "throwing caution to the wind"

- replaced "yelled happily" with *synonyms*: "shrieked with joy"

- concluded with a witchy *idiom*: "happier than a toad in a mud puddle."

Revised Narrative Handout

Names: _____

Revise the following story to be more imaginative! What shades of meaning can you add to make this more interesting to read? Don't forget—you can use similes, metaphors, synonyms, or a shade of meaning to improve the story!

I rode the bus to school. It was Tuesday. We will have gym today. It might rain.

Empowering Students' Knowledge of Vocabulary: Learning How Language Works, Grades 3–5 by Mary Jo Fresch and David L. Harrison © 2020 NCTE.

Shades of Meaning Lesson 2

"The Fox & the Grapes"

A Fox one day spied a beautiful bunch of ripe grapes hanging from a vine trained along the branches of a tree. The grapes seemed ready to <u>burst</u> with juice, and the Fox's mouth watered as he gazed longingly at them.

The bunch <u>hung</u> from a <u>high</u> branch, and the Fox had to jump for it. The first time he <u>jumped</u>, he missed it by a long way. So he walked off a short distance and took a <u>running</u> leap at it, only to fall short once more. Again and again he tried, but in vain.

Presently, he <u>sat</u> down and <u>looked at</u> the grapes in disgust.

"What a fool I am," he said. "Here I am, wearing myself out to get a bunch of sour grapes that are not worth gaping for."

And off he <u>walked</u>, very, very scornfully.

There are many who pretend to despise and belittle that which is beyond their reach.
(Source: http://www.read.gov/aesop/005.html)

Define shades of meaning:

Empowering Students' Knowledge of Vocabulary: Learning How Language Works, Grades 3–5 by Mary Jo Fresch and David L. Harrison © 2020 NCTE.

"The Ant & the Dove" Handout

Name: _____

Read the story. With your buddy, choose a new word, idiom, or metaphor to replace the underlined word. Be sure your choice still makes sense in the story.

"The Ant & the Dove"

A Dove saw an Ant <u>fall</u> into a brook. The Ant struggled in vain to reach the bank, and, in pity, the Dove dropped a blade of straw <u>close beside it</u>. Clinging to the straw like a shipwrecked sailor to a broken spar, the Ant floated safely to shore.

Soon after, the Ant saw a man getting ready to kill the Dove with a stone. But, just as he <u>cast</u> the stone, the Ant stung him in the heel, so that the pain made him miss his aim, and the startled Dove flew to safety in a <u>distant</u> wood.

A kindness is never wasted.

(Source: http://www.read.gov/aesop/028.html)

Shades of Meaning Lesson 3

Materials

- matching game cards—photocopied and cut apart to distribute, one per student

- handout—to complete with buddy

TABLE B.26. Shades of Meaning Matching Game

huge	answer	asked	end	yell
large	solution	questioned	finish	shout
happy	late	need	pair	reckless
joyous	tardy	require	duo	careless
anger	leave	right	wealth	terrified
fury	depart	correct	riches	afraid

Empowering Students' Knowledge of Vocabulary: Learning How Language Works, Grades 3–5 by Mary Jo Fresch and David L. Harrison © 2020 NCTE.

Shades of Meaning Lesson 3

Shades of Meaning Matching Game Handout

Names: _____

A. Glue your matching shades of meaning cards below:

B. Write sentences for the two words you glued above:

1. _____

2. _____

C. Discuss how your words differ, but express the same idea through shades of meaning. Write words below similar to your two words:

D. Write a sentence for one of the shades of meaning words you wrote in C (above).

1. _____

Empowering Students' Knowledge of Vocabulary: Learning How Language Works, Grades 3–5 by Mary Jo Fresch and David L. Harrison © 2020 NCTE.

Shades of Meaning Lesson 4

Word Order Handout

1. Cut apart the first column in the chart below.

2. Put the word cards in order, from less powerful to more powerful.

3. Repeat for each of the next three columns.

TABLE B.27. Word Order Cards

awesome	gobble	challenging	call
good	eat	difficult	scream
excellent	nibble	hard	yell

Empowering Students' Knowledge of Vocabulary: Learning How Language Works, Grades 3–5 by Mary Jo Fresch and David L. Harrison © 2020 NCTE.

Shades of Meaning: Independent Practice

Name: _____

Add a word on each line to show shades of meaning. For example: mad–angry–irate.

teeny–_____–small

funny–_____–hilarious

bad–_____–horrible

good–_____–terrific

happy–joyful–_____

scared–afraid–_____

sad–upset–_____

said–stated–_____

Empowering Students' Knowledge of Vocabulary: Learning How Language Works, Grades 3–5 by Mary Jo Fresch and David L. Harrison © 2020 NCTE.

Word Origin Lesson 1

"I've got a secret . . ." Which is the correct origin of these words? Can you guess?

TABLE B.28. "I've Got a Secret": Word Origins

The origin of *tulip* is:	The origin of *window* is:
A. *toul* meaning "other"	A. *winvow* meaning "hole in wall"
B. *tou lop* meaning "stand"	B. *vindr auga* meaning "wind eye"
C. *tulbend* meaning "turban"	C. *widva* meaning "see through"
D. *tullep* meaning "bloom"	D. *windee* meaning "meeting place"
The origin of *canoe* is:	The origin of *hurricane* is:
A. *casnu* meaning "to ride"	A. *hurric* meaning "to rush"
B. *kanoa* meaning "hollow log"	B. *huraca'n* meaning "center of wind"
C. *caneoe* meaning "swift"	C. *huricanne* meaning "out of control"
D. *kannol* meaning "boat"	D. *hur'a'can'o* meaning "whirling"
The origin of *globe* is:	The origin of *comet* is:
A. *globus* meaning "to roll together"	A. *commisi* meaning "picked clean"
B. *glooz* meaning "round"	B. *coemet* meaning "a bullet in the sky"
C. *globali* meaning "of the earth"	C. *kometes* meaning "having long hair"
D. *gobabli* meaning "center"	D. *commes* meaning "shining"

Empowering Students' Knowledge of Vocabulary: Learning How Language Works, Grades 3–5 by Mary Jo Fresch and David L. Harrison © 2020 NCTE.

TABLE B.29. Word Origins: Story Sheet

Tulip	In the 1500s, Austria's ambassador visited Turkey and was enchanted by the unusual flowers. The Turks' traditional name for the flower was *lale*, but the ambassador's interpreter called the blossom a *tulbend*, the Turkish word for "turban," because of its shape. When the ambassador brought home several of these exotic plants, he also brought along its picturesque nickname, *tulbend*, which slightly changed in English.
Canoe	From the Haitian, brought by Columbus, *kanoa* meaning "dugout or hollow log." When Columbus returned to Spain, the spelling changed.
Globe	From the Latin *globus*, meaning "to roll together or stick." Maps were only flat at one time, and then rolled together.
Window	When Norse carpenters built homes, they left a hole or eye in the roof to allow smoke to escape. Wind often blew through this hole and it became known as *vindr auga* meaning "wind eye."
Hurricane	Taino *huraca'n* meaning *center of the wind*. Christopher Columbus brought this word back, making its way to Spanish, and eventually English.
Comet	From the Ancient Greek *kometes* meaning "having long hair." Aristotle first used kometes to describe the heavenly body that seems to have long hair trailing from its "head." The name was later adopted into Latin as *cometes*, which eventually made its way to English.

Empowering Students' Knowledge of Vocabulary: Learning How Language Works, Grades 3–5 by Mary Jo Fresch and David L. Harrison © 2020 NCTE.

Word Origin Lesson 2

Copy this page and the next one. Cut apart the word, origin, and definition cards. Distribute to students for a partner matching game.

TABLE B.30. Word–Origin–Definition Partner Matching Game

Word	Origin	Definition
galore	Irish Gaelic *go leor*	In abundance, a lot
zero	Arabic *sifr* meaning "empty" and Middle Latin *zephirum* meaning "empty"	Mathematics symbol meaning absence of quantity
typhoon	Chinese *tai fung* meaning "big wind"	A tropical cyclone
book	Germanic *boks* meaning "beech"—the wood used for writing tablets	A written or printed work consisting of pages glued or sewn together along one side and bound in covers
funny bone	From the enlarged end of the *humerus* bone	The spot that gets a "tingly" feeling when bumped
caravan	Persian, from *karwan* meaning "company of travelers"	A group of people traveling together across a distance

TABLE B.31. Word–Origin–Definition: Story Sheet

basketball	Invented by Dr. James Naismith. A Canadian, Naismith was teaching physical education at a college in Springfield, Massachusetts, 1891. He needed an activity to keep the young men busy during the winter months. He cut the bottoms out of *peach baskets*, challenged the students to move a ball down the gym floor and throw it through the basket.	A game between two five-player teams where goals are scored by throwing the ball through a hoop at one end of a court
jeep	Abbreviation for the all-purpose vehicle developed for the military. The "general purpose" vehicle became nicknamed *g.p.*, which was shortened into a pronounceable word.	A type of vehicle
piggy bank	In the 1400s, household pots and dishes were made of cheap clay called *pygg*. Housewives would store extra coins in the "pyggy jars."	A place to save coins
school	Greek *skhole* meaning "leisure," as only rich men had the time to read and discuss ideas.	A place of learning

Empowering Students' Knowledge of Vocabulary: Learning How Language Works, Grades 3–5 by Mary Jo Fresch and David L. Harrison © 2020 NCTE.

Word Origin Lesson 3

Materials

- Fairy Tale Partner cards—copy and cut apart

TABLE B.32. Fairy Tale Partner Matching Cards

Red Riding Hood	Big Bad Wolf
Woodcutter	Grandma
Cinderella	Fairy Godmother
Stepsister	Prince
Goldilocks	Papa Bear
Mama Bear	Baby Bear
Snow White	Sneezy
Doc	Sleepy
Jack	Beanstalk
Giant	Goose with the golden egg
Sleeping Beauty	Witch
Poison apple	Prince

Empowering Students' Knowledge of Vocabulary: Learning How Language Works, Grades 3–5 by Mary Jo Fresch and David L. Harrison © 2020 NCTE.

Materials

- word origin tree—our tree artwork was downloaded from Pixabay (https://pixabay.com), a website offering royalty- and permission-free photos and images

Project this example:

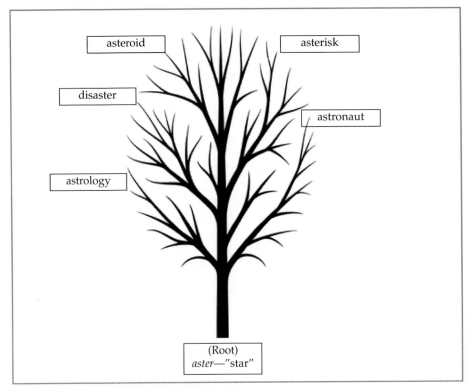

FIGURE B.2. Sample word origin tree (image source: https://pixabay.com).

- asteroid—*aster* (star) + *oid* (shape) = star shape
- disaster—*dis* (bad) + *aster* (star) = bad star (people thought they were under a "bad star" if they had a disaster)
- astrology—*aster* (star) + *ology* (study of) = study of the stars
- asterisk—*aster* (star; from Greek *asteriskos*) = little star
- astronaut—*aster* (star) + *naut* (sailor) = star sailor

Enlarge the image of the tree and make six copies. Write each of the following roots and its meaning in one of the boxes labeled "root":

1. *graph*—to write
2. *sign*—to mark
3. *tract*—to pull or drag
4. *cent*—hundred
5. *port*—to carry
6. *meter*—measure

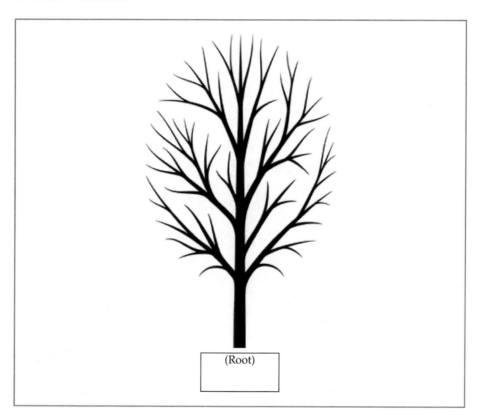

(Root)

FIGURE B.3. Blank word origin tree (image source: https://pixabay.com).

Word Origins: Independent Practice

Name: _____

Choose one or more of the following activities:

1. Find Austria and Turkey on a map. How might the ambassador have traveled in the 1500s? Describe his journey and route.

2. Find a picture of a canoe. How does a modern-day canoe look like a hollow log?

3. Draw what a Norse "wind eye" would have looked like. Now draw your own window.

4. Who were the Taino people that Christopher Columbus met and learned the word *huraca'n* from?

5. Look up the name and picture of a comet. Which did you find? Does it look like it has "long hair?"

Empowering Students' Knowledge of Vocabulary: Learning How Language Works, Grades 3–5 by Mary Jo Fresch and David L. Harrison © 2020 NCTE.

Appendix C

Electronic Resources for Teachers

- www.allwords.com—this online dictionary does a multilingual search that ELL students will find very useful; "links for word lovers" will take you to all kinds of resources for information (dictionaries, thesaurus, etymologies) and wordplay (puns, rhymes, songs, quotations)

- www.armoredpenguin.com/wordsearch—you can use the "generator" to create your own word jumbles and puzzles

- www.askoxford.com—this online dictionary includes word games and other support materials for spelling, grammar, etymology, and foreign phrases, plus an "ask the experts" link through which you can find answers to frequently asked questions about language

- www.behindthename.com—research the meaning and origin of names; this is a good place to begin word histories by having students find their own name's meaning

- www.brainpop.com/english—free access to activities related to synonyms, antonyms, and homonyms

- www.esldesk.com/esl-quizzes/frequently-used-english-words/words.htm—provides, in increments of 300, the 1,000 most frequently used words in English

- www.factmonster.com/ipka/A0907017.html—provides lists of Latin and Greek roots

- funbrain.com/content/detect—you or your students enter a list of words that Fun Brain hides in a puzzle; students can choose skill level and play alone or with a friend; also has puzzles based on some children's literature

- www.fun-with-words.com/etymology.html—this etymological resource provides histories of common words and idioms

Empowering Students' Knowledge of Vocabulary: Learning How Language Works, Grades 3–5 by Mary Jo Fresch and David L. Harrison © 2020 NCTE.

- journeynorth.org/tm/vocab.html—Journey North has quick and easy classroom activities that combine science and vocabulary building

- www.nwp.org/cs/public/print/resource/quarterly/Q2002no3/sim mons.html—this article comes from the National Writing Project WWW site; it describes several activities that foster word learning and practice through illustrations

- www.onelook.com—type in a word and let this site look it up in several dictionaries; it also has a "Reverse Dictionary," in which you type in a description of a concept and it finds words and phrases that match it

- pbskids.org/games/vocabulary—the PBS Kids site includes multiple entertaining games to support vocabulary development with young children's favorite characters

- www.literacymatters.org—includes links to lesson plans for content vocabulary, "tools" for teaching vocabulary, strategy descriptions, and general vocabulary activities

- www.merriam-webster.com—this site has an extensive and easy-to-use online dictionary and thesaurus that even provides audio pronunciations; students will enjoy free word games and can sign up for the "Word of the Day" feature

- www.readingrockets.org/atoz/vocabulary—the Reading Rockets vocabulary page includes articles for parents and teachers, videos, research, activities, blogs, connections to digital literacy opportunities, and more

- readwritethink.org—this site, sponsored by NCTE, contains lesson plans for all aspects of the language arts and at all grade levels; to find vocabulary plans, select "Learning about Language" and then "Vocabulary"; you can also narrow your search by selecting a grade-level band

- www.rif.org—Reading is Fundamental provides many resources for teachers and parents; Literacy Central has interactive games, songs, activities and reading to support the development of language skills; these are in both English and Spanish

- www.superkids.com/aweb/tools/words/search—make your own printable hidden word puzzles using the "Puzzle Creator"

- www.thesaurus.com—type in a word and quickly find synonyms and antonyms; also has a dictionary, an encyclopedia, and a word-of-the-day in English and Spanish

- www.tv411.org/vocabulary—a variety of vocabulary lessons that can be used online

- www.virtualsalt.com/roots.htm—lists roots and words that come from them
- www.wordorigins.org—explains the origin of more than 400 familiar words and phrases that are "interesting or because some bit of folklore, sometimes true and sometimes false, is associated with the origin"
- www.wordsmith.org/words/today.html—can be set up to email a new word to you every day; also provides a vocabulary word, its definition, pronunciation information (with audio clip), etymology, usage example, and a quotation

Appendix D

Electronic Resources for Students

- Amby's Education Resources for Reading and Vocabulary (amby.com/educate/reading.html)—several interesting games for students

- Ed.Helper.com (www.edhelper.com)—lesson ideas for across the curriculum

- Game Zone (www.english-online.org.uk/games/gamezone2.htm)—a variety of games, some more related to grammar than vocabulary

- Learning Vocabulary Can Be Fun! (www.vocabulary.co.il)—for all age and "skill" levels; students can play the "match game" and "hangman" or do crossword puzzles, word searches, and jumbles; all the activities are for one player

- Little Explorers English Picture Dictionary (www.enchantedlearning.com/Dictionary.html)—when students click on a letter of the alphabet, they will find dozens of words, each with a picture and definition; best of all, this site also has picture dictionaries that go from English to Spanish, French, Italian, Portuguese, German, Swedish, Dutch, and Japanese; these dictionaries will captivate all your students and provide extra support to ELL students

- The Problem Site (www.theproblemsite.com/word_games.asp)—provides multiple word games to assist in vocabulary development

- Surfing the Net with Kids (www.surfnetkids.com/games)—lots of free kids' games listed by type (e.g., crossword, jigsaw), topic (e.g., science, geography), or theme (e.g., sports, dress-up, holidays); the site also has an easy-to-use search tool

- Word Central (www.wordcentral.com)—maintained by Merriam-Webster, this site has plenty of activities and information for students, as well as resources (including lesson plans) for teachers; you can even build your own dictionary.

Empowering Students' Knowledge of Vocabulary: Learning How Language Works, Grades 3–5 by Mary Jo Fresch and David L. Harrison © 2020 NCTE.

Appendix E

Resources about and for ELL Students

Print Resources

- *Academic Language for English Language Learners and Struggling Readers: How To Help Students Succeed across Content Areas* (Freeman & Freeman, 2008)—reports current research and effective instructional ideas for teaching academic language skills for middle and secondary students

- *Making Content Comprehensible for Elementary English Learners: The SIOP Model* (Echevarria et al., 2010)—provides many instructional ideas for supporting academic language development and making content comprehensible

- *Teaching Vocabulary to English Language Learners* (Graves et al., 2012)—offers a plan for vocabulary instruction for ELLs focused on providing rich and varied language experiences.

Electronic Resources

- www.allwords.com—the online dictionary does a multilingual search that ELL students will find very useful; "links for word lovers" will take you to all kinds of resources for information (dictionaries, thesaurus, etymologies) and wordplay (puns, rhymes, songs, quotations)

- www.colorincolorado.org/educators/teaching/vocabulary—the Colorín Colorado site provides many resources for supporting ELLs; this particular page includes effective classroom strategies for supporting vocabulary development

- www.cultofpedagogy.com/supporting-esl-students-mainstream-classroom—suggests "12 ways to Support English Learners in the Mainstream Classroom"

Empowering Students' Knowledge of Vocabulary: Learning How Language Works, Grades 3–5 by Mary Jo Fresch and David L. Harrison © 2020 NCTE.

- www.ego4u.com—this website provides rules of grammar, vocabulary exercises, and writing rules; although intended for ELL students, benefits can be gained by non-ELL students as well

- www.enchantedlearning.com/Dictionary.html—when they click on a letter of the alphabet, students will find dozens of words, each with a picture and definition; best of all, this site also has multiple dual-language picture dictionaries; these dictionaries will captivate all your students and provide extra support to ELLs; note that older students may enjoy working with some of the other electronic dictionaries and resources listed in the Resources for Teachers section

- www.englishclub.com/esl-games/matching.htm—intended for ELL students, the website focuses on matching synonyms and antonyms, but includes general knowledge matching games as well; note that matching games feature words in isolation

- www.eslcafe.com—lots of resources for teachers and students alike at Dave's ESL (English as a Second Language) Café

- eslgold.com/build-vocabulary—a variety of "highly recommended" vocabulary links

- www.manythings.org/lulu—includes English vocabulary games with pictures (word to picture/picture to word); the images and words are for beginning students; the topics include animals, transportation, food and drink, clothing, and many others

- www.totalesl.com—from the homepage, click on "Total ESL Resources" and then scroll down to different resources; resources include ELL language arts, literature, and online games; most resources are sorted by grade level

- www.wida.wisc.edu—the WIDA (via the Wisconsin Center for Education Research) website is focused on supporting academic language development for ELLs; the site includes information on standards and instruction, assessment, professional development, and research

References

Abel, B. (2003). English idioms in the first language and second language lexicon: A dual representation approach. *Second Language Research, 19*(4), 329–358. https://doi.org/10.1191/0267658303sr226oa

Berne, J. I., & Blachowicz, C. L. Z. (2008). What reading teachers say about vocabulary instruction: Voices from the classroom. *The Reading Teacher, 62*(4), 314–323. https://doi.org/10.1598/RT.62.4.4

Bhalla, J. (2009). *I'm not hanging noodles on your ears: And other intriguing idioms from around the world.* National Geographic Society.

Blachowicz, C. L. Z., & Fisher, P. (2004). Vocabulary lessons. *Educational Leadership, 61*(6), 66–69. http://www.educationalleader.com/subtopicintro/read/ASCD/ASCD_352_1.pdf

Blachowicz, C. L. Z., & Fisher, P. J. (2014). *Teaching vocabulary in all classrooms* (5th ed.). Pearson.

Blachowicz, C. L. Z., Fisher, P. J., Ogle, D., & Watts-Taffe, S. (2006). Vocabulary: Questions from the classroom. *Reading Research Quarterly, 41*(4), 524–539. https://doi.org/10.1598/RRQ.41.4.5

Brown, D. (2001). *Deception point.* Simon & Schuster.

Bruner, J. (2002). *Making stories: Law, literature, life.* Farrar, Straus and Giroux.

Caillies, S., & Le Sourn-Bissaoui, S. (2008). Children's understanding of idioms and theory of mind development. *Developmental Science, 11*(5), 703–711. https://doi.org/10.1111/j.1467-7687.2008.00720.x

Cain, K., Oakhill, J., & Lemmon, K. (2005). The relation between children's reading comprehension level and their comprehension of idioms. *Journal of Experimental Child Psychology, 90*(1), 65–87. https://doi.org/10.1016/j.jecp.2004.09.003

Culham, R. (2005). *6 + 1 traits of writing: The complete guide for the primary grades.* Scholastic.

Echevarria, J., Vogt, M., & Short, D. J. (2010). *Making content comprehensible for elementary English learners: The SIOP model.* Pearson.

Fenker, D., & Schütze, H. (2008, December 17). Learning by surprise. *Scientific American.* https://www.scientificamerican.com/article/learning-by-surprise

Freeman, Y., & Freeman, D. (2008). *Academic language for English language learners and struggling readers: How to help students succeed across content areas.* Heinemann.

Fresch, M. J. (2014). *Engaging minds in English language arts classrooms: The surprising power of joy.* ASCD.

Graham, A. K. (1976). Sally. In D. F. Haas (Ed.), *The Witchbook* (M. Ranft, Illus.) (pp. 48–57). Rand McNally.

Graves, M. F., August, D., & Mancilla-Martinez, J. (2012). *Teaching vocabulary to English language learners.* Teachers College Press.

Graves, M. F., Juel, C., Graves, B. B., & Dewitz, P. (2010). *Teaching reading in the 21st century: Motivating all learners* (5th ed.). Allyn & Bacon.

Hansen, J., Richland, L. E., Baumer, E. P. S., & Tomlinson, W. (2011, April 8–12). Metaphor and creativity in learning science [Paper presentation]. American Educational Research Association Annual Meeting, New Orleans, LA. https://www.ics.uci.edu/~wmt/pubs/Tomlinson_CF17.pdf

Harrison, D. L., & Fresch, M. J. (2018). *7 keys to research for writing success.* Scholastic.

The Idioms. (2019). *The idioms: Largest idiom dictionary.* https://www.theidioms.com

Johnson, D. D., Johnson, B. V. H., & Schlichting, K. (2004). Logology: Word and language play. In J. F. Baumann & E. J. Kame'enui (Eds.), *Vocabulary instruction: Research to practice* (pp. 179–200). Guilford.

Kelley, J. G., Lesaux, N. K., Kieffer, M. J., & Faller, S. E. (2010). Effective academic vocabulary instruction in the urban middle school. *The Reading Teacher, 64*(1), 5–14. https://doi.org/10.1598/RT.64.1.1

Kinney, J. (2007). *Diary of a wimpy kid.* Amulet.

Kostadinovska-Stojckevska, B. (2018). The semantic aspect of the acquisition of synonyms, homonyms, and antonyms in the teaching process of English as a foreign language. *European Journal of Foreign Language Teaching, 3*(2), 28–43. https://doi.org/10.5281/zenodo.1216500

Laflamme, J. G. (1997). The effect of multiple exposure vocabulary method and the target reading/writing strategy on test scores. *Journal of Adolescent & Adult Literacy, 40*(5), 372–384.

Lederer, R. (2019). Richard Lederer's verbivore. http://verbivore.com/wordpress

Literary Devices. (2019). *Types of analogy.* http://www.literarydevices.com/analogy

Loewen, N. (2011). *"You're toast" and other metaphors we adore.* Picture Window Books.

Lundblom, E. E. G., & Woods, J. J. (2012). Working in the classroom: Improving idiom comprehension through classwide peer tutoring. *Communication Disorders Quarterly, 33*(4), 202–219. https://doi.org/10.1177/1525740111404927

Lynch, M. (2019, February 22). 6 key ingredients of student engagement. *The Edvocate.* https://www.theedadvocate.org/6-key-ingredients-of-student-engagement

Merriam-Webster. (1993a). Expedition. In *Webster's third new international dictionary* (p. 799).

Merriam-Webster. (1993b). Coconut. In *Webster's third new international dictionary* (p. 437).

Mountain, L. (2002). Flip-a-Chip to build vocabulary. *Journal of Adolescent and Adult Literacy*, *46*(1), 62–68. https://doi.org/10.1598/JAAL.46.1.7

National Assessment of Educational Progress. (2012). *Vocabulary summary*. The Nation's Report Card: Vocabulary results from the 2009 and 2011 NAEP Reading Assessments. https://www.nationsreportcard.gov/reading_2011/voc_summary.aspx

National Council of Teachers of English. (1992, June 1). *Teaching storytelling: A position statement from the Committee on Storytelling, 1992.* https://ncte.org/statement/teaching storytelling

National Institute of Child Health and Human Development. (2000). *Report of the National Reading Panel: Teaching children to read: An evidence-based assessment of the scientific research literature on reading and its implications for reading instruction* (NIH Publication No. 00-4769). United States Government Printing Office.

Piven, H. (2010). *My best friend is as sharp as a pencil.* Schwartz & Wade.

Piven, H. (2012). *My dog is as smelly as dirty socks.* Dragonfly Books.

Ringstad, A. (2013a). *The compelling histories of long arm of the law and other idioms* (D. McGeehan, Illus.). The Child's World.

Ringstad, A. (2013b). *The over-the-top histories of chew the scenery and other idioms* (D. McGeehan, Illus.). The Child's World.

Simpson, R., & Mendis, D. (2003). A corpus-based study of idioms in academic speech. *TESOL Quarterly*, *37*(3), 419–441. https://doi.org/10.2307/3588398

Terban, M. (2007). *In a pickle and other funny idioms* (G. Maestro, Illus.). HMH Books for Young Readers.

Terban, M. (2008). *Scholastic dictionary of idioms.* Scholastic.

Whitaker, S. R. (2008). *Word play: Building vocabulary.* Heinemann.

Wong, J. S. (2018). Poetry Fridays. In S. Vardell & J. Wong (Eds.), *GREAT morning! Poems for school leaders to read aloud* (p. 17). Pomelo Books.

Yolen, J. (1987). *Owl moon.* Philomel Books.

Index

Ferris wheel, term origin, 19
Fisher, P. J., 36, 69
flying colors, term origin, 56
"The Fox & the Grapes" story, 74–75, 139

Ghigna, Charles, 84–86, 94
globe, term origin, 145
Grimes, Nikki, 92–93, 96
Grouping game, 61–62, 126
guy, term origin, 19

Hansen, J., 50
homographs, meaning of, 8, 21
homonyms
    meaning of, 8, 21
    number of, 10
    purpose of learning, 21
    types of, 8
homonyms lessons, homographs
    "Homographs" (poem), 24, 105
    "In a Jam" (poem), 24–25, 105–6
    independent practice, 26
    listed, 97
    "A Peculiar Event" (poem), 25–26, 107
    write a poem, 26
homonyms lessons, homophones
    "Homophones" (poem), 22, 104
    independent practice, 26
    listed, 97
    "The Party" (chart), 23, 104
    riddles, 26, 107
homophones, meaning of, 8
"How to Build a Poem" (Ghigna), 84–85
hurricane, term origin, 145

idioms
    academic importance of, 52–53
    in advertising, 6
    conclusion, 66–67
    in conversations, 56–57
    decomposable vs. nondecomposable, 52
    in fiction, 51
    globally, 51–52
    making new, 57–58
    meaning of, 52

number of, 53
origins of, researching and creating, 56, 58
purpose of learning, 58
recognizing, 54–55
teacher's perspective on, 52–53
term origin, 52
writer's perspective on, 54–58
idioms lessons
    Afternoon Idiom Challenge, 67
    defining and using idioms, 60–61, 64, 124
    Grouping game, 61–62, 126
    Idioms, Meanings, and Origins game, 61, 125
    Idioms-Story chart, 64, 131
    illustrating idioms, 64, 128
    independent practice, 66
    investigating idioms, 62, 127
    listed, 98
    Make Your Own Idioms, 65, 132–33
    origins of, researching and creating, 64, 129–30
    readers theater, 135
"In a Jam" (Harrison), 24–25, 105–6
inference, example, 68
instruction, vocabulary. *See also* resources
    context clues in, 68
    methods, 2–3
    traditional, 6
"Invention-Retronym" (Harrison), 28–29, 109
I've Got a Secret chart, 80, 144–45

jeep, term origin, 146
jumbo, term origin, 19

King, Stephen, 89

Le Sourn-Bissaoui, S., 52
Lynch, M., 4

"The Magic of Metaphors!" (Ghigna), 84–86
Make Your Own Idioms, 65, 132–33
Matching Game
    acronyms lessons, 12–13, 99

Authors

Mary Jo Fresch is an academy professor and professor emerita in the School of Teaching and Learning, College of Education and Human Ecology, at The Ohio State University. She has been an educator for more than forty years. She began her teaching career as a third-grade teacher, and then worked with adults with challenging literacy needs at the University of Akron. She has spent the last thirty years teaching literacy courses for preservice and inservice teachers at the University of Nebraska (Lincoln), the Royal  Melbourne Institute and Deakin University (both in Melbourne, Australia), and The Ohio State University. She speaks nationally and internationally about literacy-related topics. Her research focuses on the developmental aspect of literacy learning. She has over sixty peer-reviewed articles in professional journals such as *Language Arts, Journal of Literacy Research, The Reading Teacher, Reading and Writing Quarterly*, and *Reading Psychology*. Her professional books include *Strategies for Effective Balanced Literacy* (2016), *The Power of Picture Books: Using Content Area Literature in Middle School* (2009), *Engaging Minds in English Language Arts Classrooms: The Surprising Power of Joy* (2014), and *An Essential History of Current Reading Practices* (editor; 2008). She coauthored *Learning through Poetry* (2013), a five-book phonemic and phonological awareness series, and *7 Keys to Research for Writing Success* (2018) with David L. Harrison. Fresch continues to provide professional learning workshops for teachers across the United States. She is married to her college sweetheart (Hank), has two married children, and five grandchildren.

David L. Harrison has published more than 100 books of poetry, fiction, and nonfiction for young readers and teachers, and has been anthologized in 185 others. His work has been translated into twelve languages and presented on television, radio, podcast, video stream, on stage, and in musical groups. Harrison's professional books include *Easy Poetry Lessons That Dazzle and Delight* (1999), with Bernice Cullinan; "Yes, Poetry Can," the poetry chapter for *Children's Literature in the Reading Program* (edited by  Deborah Wooten, Lauren Almonette Liang, and Bernice Cullinan, third [2009], fourth [2015], and fifth [2018] editions); *Learning through Poetry* (2013), with Mary Jo Fresch, a five-volume set to build phonemic awareness and phonics skills; and *Partner Poems for Building Fluency: 40 Engaging Poems for Two Voices with Motivating Activities That Help Students Improve Their Fluency and Comprehension* (2009), with Tim Rasinski and Gay Fawcett. *Let's Write This Week with David Harrison* (2012), with Lauren Edmondson, is a 20-episode video program that brings writing tips into the elementary classroom. Harrison holds degrees from Drury and Emory Universities and honorary doctorates of letters from Missouri State University and Drury University. David Harrison Elementary School is named in his honor. He is poet laureate of Drury University. In 2020 he became the first recipient of the Laura Ingalls Wilder Children's Literature Medal.

This book was typeset in TheMix and Palatino by Barbara Frazier.

Typefaces used on the cover include ITC Lubalin Graph and Myriad Pro.

The book was printed on 50-lb. White Offset paper by Seaway Printing Company, Inc.